Happiness in the Home

Guidelines for Spouses and Parents

Harold Hazelip

BAKER BOOK HOUSE
Grand Rapids, Michigan 49506

Copyright 1985 by
Baker Book House Company

ISBN: 0-8010-4294-1

Printed in the United States of America

The author is grateful to the following publishers who gave permission to reprint excerpts from selected materials:

Achtemeier, Elizabeth Rice: *The Committed Marriage.* Philadelphia, PA, The Westminster Press, 1976.

Briggs, Dorothy Corkille: *Your Child's Self-Esteem.* Garden City, NY, Dolphin Books: a Division of Doubleday & Company, Inc. Copyright 1970 by Dorothy Corkille Briggs.

Buechner, Frederick: *Wishful Thinking.* New York, Harper & Row Publishers, Inc. 1973.

Clinebell, Howard J., Jr. and Clinebell, Charlotte H.: *The Intimate Marriage.* New York, Harper & Row Publishers, Inc. Copyright 1970 by Howard J. Clinebell, Jr., and Charlotte H. Clinebell.

Curran, Dolores: *Traits of a Healthy Family.* Minneapolis, Winston Press. Copyright 1983 by Dolores Curran.

Drescher, John M.: *If I Were Starting My Family Again.* Nashville, TN, Festival Books: a Division of Abingdon Press, 1979.

Fitzgerald, F. Scott: *The Great Gatsby.* New York, Charles Scribner's Sons, 1925. Renewal copyright 1953 by Frances Scott Fitzgerald Lanahan.

Felleman, Hazel: *The Best Loved Poems* (Tarkington, F. "The Land of Beginning Again"). Garden City, NY, Doubleday & Company, Inc., 1936.

Hechinger, Grace and Fred M.: *Teen-Age Tyranny.* New York, William Morrow and Co., Inc./Publishers. Copyright 1962 by Grace Hechinger and Fred M. Hechinger.

Kesler, Kay: *Parents & Teenagers.* Wheaton, IL, Victor Books, 1984. Copyright 1984 by Youth for Christ/USA.

McGinnis, Alan Loy: *The Friendship Factor.* Minneapolis, Augsburg Publishing House, 1979.

Peppler, Alice Stolper: *Single Again—This Time with Children.* Minneapolis, Augsburg Publishing House, 1982.

Roman, Mel and Raley, Patricia: *The Indelible Family.* New York, Rawson Associates, 1980.

Tocqueville, Alexis de (translated by Henry Reeve): *Democracy in America,* Vol. II. New York, Alfred A. Knopf, 1945. Used by permission of Random House, Inc./Alfred A. Knopf, Inc.

Winn, Marie: *Children Without Childhood.* New York, Pantheon Books: a Division of Random House, Inc. Copyright 1981 by Marie Winn.

To **Helen, Pat, Jeff, Cheryl**
They have taught me what happiness in the home is.

Contents

Preface

For more than three decades I have officiated at weddings. I have seen young couples look deeply into each other's eyes and make promises intended to last for life. And many of them have!

I have increasingly come to believe that certain principles enhance a marriage and a family and that the absence of these basic values endangers a family relationship. I regularly talk with young couples about these convictions prior to their wedding.

The first essential is commitment. Marriage is an ongoing working relationship between two people, and only those who genuinely determine to stay together will make it. A central value system is important in achieving that goal. Specifically, I refer to Christian faith held in common by both partners.

Communication heads the list of traits of the happy family in most of the recent studies I have seen. This implies the desire to understand more than to be understood. Further, I believe that integrity—fidelity—is even more vital to marriage than the vague term *love*.

These values will be explored in this attempt to point toward *Happiness in the Home*. And they will be applied to the challenges of parenting as well as the junctures of married life.

Several people have provided me with valuable input as these chapters were written. Randy Becton helped to originate the idea for these studies. Tony Ash, Doug Brown, Jr., Bill Flatt, Joel Johnson, Stan Reid, Harold Shank, and Charles Siburt have helped with suggestions and/or research. James Thompson has been especially helpful with research assistance. Annie May Lewis has made stylistic suggestions, and Jane Tomlinson has typed the manuscript. I am indebted to each of them.

1

What Is a Family?

In 1979 the President of the United States convened the White House Conference on the Family. The purpose of the conference was to do something about the increasing instability of the family and provide some answers to the question, "What is happening to the family?" Religious leaders, social activists, and political figures were asked to study the family and make recommendations for strengthening its structure and influence.

Those who attended quickly discovered that they could not agree on the most basic question: What is a family? Although most of the participants had grown up in families, their experiences had been so different that they could not agree on what families looked like. They agreed that the family is a "good thing," but could agree on little else.

What is a family? Is it that harmonious unit we have seen on the "Waltons," complete with three generations and lots of happiness? Is it also represented by the single parent who tries to combine making a living with the

rearing of children? What about the married couple who
has chosen to have no children in order to pursue their
respective careers? Is it the couple who has chosen to
live together without any binding commitments? All of
those views of the family were represented at the White
House Conference.

The Changing Family Structure

Stanley Hauerwas, a professor of ethics at an American university, teaches a popular course in family life.
In his book *A Community of Character*, he tells of students who come to his class looking for helpful hints on
improving family life. He especially likes to ask them
this question: Why have children? Hauerwas usually
finds students have never considered the question before. They know that the traditional family is made up
of Mom and Dad and the children, but they find the
question difficult. Some say, "Children are fun." Or,
"Children come as an expression of a couple's love." Or,
"Having children is just the thing to do." But they
wonder whether any of these are adequate reasons for
having children.

It is when you ask, "Why have children?" that you are
getting to the heart of what kind of family you want to
have. (We will leave aside the couple who may choose
not to have children because of some special mission
that they believe they can best fulfill alone. Nor will we
address the couple who are physically unable to have
children.) Have you thought of the economic and emotional costs of having children? In one sense, they take
away our freedom from the moment they are born. In
their earliest days, they awaken us in the night with
cries for food and attention. They limit our freedom of
movement, our ability to meet schedules. As they grow,
their demands do not lessen, much less cease. Children
are vulnerable. They get sick and have problems in

school. And they need you. As long as you live, you will be anxious about them. Indeed, why have children?

We have all heard the prediction that the family will become obsolete and unneeded, but I do not believe this. It may be true that almost half of today's marriages end in divorce. But 76 percent of divorced people remarry, half of them within three years. The result is that we have "blended families," where the children of two separate marriages live together in one house. Most people do not stop living in a family unit for most of their lives.

Even those who try to live without a traditional family end up in relationships that look very much like a family. The question really is: What kind of family do you want? Are you satisfied with an arrangement whereby two or more people share the same address and go their separate ways? Do you want a family where each person is there only temporarily? Or do you want something more?

It is true that sweeping changes are taking place in American family life. Many children spend more time in day-care centers than with their parents. In some families, freedom is so important that husbands and wives may be committed more to their own fulfillment than to the interests of the family unit. Either spouse may give more concern to a career than to the child or the marriage partner.

In other families, two people may choose not to have children because they do not wish to be burdened. They would like to be free to grab every enjoyment that life has to offer—the vacations, the freedoms, the luxuries. And children would be an obstacle to this fulfillment.

Commitment to Another

Although such couples are families, they seem to lack the most essential ingredients of what a family can be. I believe that a family is infinitely more than two or more people physically sharing the same household while pursuing their own interests. What it means to be a family is most beautifully expressed when two people accept all the risks of having children, knowing that they will always be "on call." The fullest human life is one that takes a chance on being committed to another human being. Parents have the rare opportunity to give love, to sacrifice themselves, to look out for someone else—all of those things that make us human.

I have seen parents beam with pride when their son or daughter crossed the stage at a school graduation. I have been thrilled by my own children at the milestones along the way—the first words, the first steps, graduation, the honors received. Such achievements help to make being a parent worthwhile.

But this is not all that makes parenting meaningful. I also know parents who give generously in the most adverse circumstances. I have seen parents of a retarded child adjust their schedules and lives to fit the special needs of their child. I have seen parents sacrifice career advancement because a child was struck with a chronic disease. I have watched them build their lives around the child, never complaining about their loss of freedom. Such parents can tell us most about what it means to be a family.

Do you recall those words in the wedding ceremony, "For better or for worse, in sickness and in health, until death do us part"? A man and a woman make that vow together, but the same words are also appropriate when a child is born. To bring a child into the world is to say, "I will care for you—whether you win the Heisman Trophy or whether you live always with a mental or physical handicap. I will love you, regardless of whether you are an honor student or are unable to compete with others scholastically. I will love you as a part of myself. If necessary, I will sacrifice my own ambitions for your sake."

Let me try my hand at answering my own questions. Why get married? Why have children? Granted, if I do either to satisfy a selfish ambition, I will have an unhappy family or one that cannot last. But there are better reasons for having a family. I want a family because God has planted in me the intense need to love and care for someone else. I discover the most fulfilling life not when I grab every moment of pleasure for myself, but when I lose myself in the needs of another person. Jesus said it: "He who loses his life . . . will find it" (Matt. 10:39). Nothing matters more in life than caring. And the family offers me that special opportunity.

Have you thought of what it is that holds a family together? Is it a matter of discovering the right mate? Having the right children? I believe a family is held together by such words as duty, obligation, commitment, honor, mutual aid, and support. Christopher Lasch has written a recent book on the family titled *Haven in a Heartless World.* The family may be the one place on earth where you can be accepted when you seem to have made a wreck of your life, the one sanctuary where you are valued when you are old. The one refuge where you have worth when you can no longer produce. What holds a family together is the promise— "For better or for worse, in sickness and in health, until death do us part."

Sy Silverberg is a therapist in Toronto who has counseled with thousands of couples who have experimented with the alternatives to family life. After observing the wreckage in many of these lives, Silverberg concluded:

> Man must have long-term relationships. . . . He must believe that there is someone who will accept and continue to care. You can't accomplish that with someone in a casual or temporary commitment. As long as one craves for permanence in his life, he will seek marriage.

There is no acceptable alternative to the family.

In the Bible, a Family Is . . .

When I try to define "family," I think of several paragraphs in the New Testament that tell us about living in a genuine family. Some of these paragraphs were written to show parents and their children how Jesus Christ alters family life. Others were written to communities of Christians who had come together to form a new family of God.

The first example is from Ephesians: "For this reason I bow my knees before the Father, from whom every family in heaven and on earth is named" (Eph. 3:14, 15). This is a beautiful reminder that all the families on earth came into being because of the One who has revealed himself as our Father. When we look to him, we understand what it means to be a father. God is not a tyrant, nor is he negligent and unloving. He is the Father who cares so much for his children that he shares their pain and provides for their needs.

Jesus gave us an insight into family life when he told the story of the prodigal son who left home and disappointed his father. The son wasted his inheritance and brought shame on his family. But Jesus' story leaves etched in our memory the forgiving father who ran to welcome his wayward son (Luke 15:11–24). Jesus was saying, "This is what God is like." Instead of demanding justice when we disappoint him, he offers a way to return. The Father goes on loving, even when we hurt him deeply.

The Bible also uses other images. God is the Bridegroom. He has chosen his bride, the church, and will love and care for her forever. But the bride is often unfaithful. Her attention span is short. She forgets her indebtedness and commitment to the Groom. The Bridegroom goes on loving forever, waiting for the bride to return home (Hos. 2, 3).

So Paul says that "every family in heaven and on

earth" gets its name from God. The Father has shown us what it means to live in a family. He is the Father whose love will not let us go.

A second paragraph that describes what it means to live in a family is in 1 Corinthians. Paul tells a new congregation what it means to live together: "If one member suffers, all suffer together; if one member is honored, all rejoice together" (1 Cor. 12:26). In the family, as in the church, we share each other's disappointments and joys.

I almost never perform a wedding without reading Paul's description of love in 1 Corinthians 13: "Love is patient and kind; love is not jealous or boastful; it is not arrogant or rude. Love does not insist on its own way; it is not irritable or resentful; it does not rejoice at wrong, but rejoices in the right. Love bears all things, believes all things, hopes all things, endures all things. Love never ends . . ." (1 Cor. 13:4–8). Although those words were written to tell Christians how to live together in community, they also have special meaning for the family. We never keep score of personal injuries or of little favors. The family is the place where "love bears all things."

In a third passage, Jesus was talking to men and women about their responsibilities to the family. He recalled the fifth commandment: "Honor your father and mother" (Mark 7:10). These words were originally spoken to middle-aged couples about their respect for their aged parents. Those couples had responsibilities toward their own families—earning a living, caring for their children. Jesus reminded them that those who leave home to form their own families are never to forget to honor their fathers and their mothers.

What is a family? A family is a place where you can grow old with dignity, knowing you will not be forgotten. The victims of today's revolution in family life are not only the children whose care is left to various institutions and parental substitutes. The victims are also aged parents whose lives would be brighter if they could interact with their children and grandchildren. And those children and grandchildren need the experience of showing appreciation for the wisdom and experience of those who are growing old.

A fourth biblical paragraph was written to show new Christians what a difference Christ makes in family life. Is a Christian family different from any other family? Peter's answer is "Yes!"—". . . wives, be submissive to your husbands. . . . husbands, live considerately with your wives, bestowing honor on the woman as the weaker sex, since you are joint heirs of the grace of life, in order that your prayers may not be hindered" (1 Peter 3:1, 7).

What is a Christian family? It is a small community where Jesus Christ makes all the difference. Here husbands and wives pray together. They are mindful of the story of Jesus, the One who gave himself for others. There is no struggle to dominate, no grab for power. There is mutual love and respect as the story of the cross teaches the husband and wife the value of living for someone else.

What kind of family do you want? The Bible offers powerful insights on what makes a genuine family. It all begins when you learn to care for others as God has cared for you.

2

A Listener's Guide
to a Happier Home

Sinclair Lewis's novel *Main Street* tells of a young wife named Carol Kennicott who moved with her doctor husband to Gopher Prairie, Minnesota. She had idealistic goals for family and community living, but she found that no one was really interested in developing a relationship with her. She hungered for communication with other women, for intimacy with her husband, for a deep concern in her family, but she came up empty-handed.

Carol Kennicott represented an isolated cry for relationship in this 1920 novel. However, anyone listening to the sounds of the current American scene is well aware that many people today—husbands, wives, children—idenfity with her yearnings. Family Service America found that 87 percent of the families in one of its surveys have difficulty in communicating, even with loved ones.

Dolores Curran reports in *Traits of a Healthy Family* that "communicating and listening" was selected as the number-one characteristic of happy families by the more than 500 professionals she consulted. Many marriage-and-family counselors report that the single most familiar complaint in unhappy marriages is that the couple no longer communicates with each other. Meanwhile, children complain that their parents do not really listen to them, as mothers and fathers likewise find their offspring ignoring what *they* say.

The Desire to Communicate

John Drakeford tells in *The Awesome Power of the Listening Ear* of a guessing game that one woman played before her own marriage. When on a dinner date, she would try to decide whether other couples around her were married. She concluded that married couples either ate in silence or with the woman talking furiously to an unresponsive husband. This amateur psychologist decided that lack of communication was the best indicator of marriage!

What happens to our willingness or ability to communicate, once we are married? During dating and the early months of marriage, romance tends to dominate the relationship. These are great days of discovery, adventure, and conversation. Mutual dreams for life are stretched out before the couple. No obstacle is too high. Tight budgets, cramped living conditions, and personal adjustments are all part of the exciting challenge.

Then comes stage two. The couple settles down to the business of living. Serious about getting ahead, each begins to scramble for the symbols of success. She is exhausted by her duties as cook, maintenance expert, wife, mother, and perhaps an outside job. His world of work becomes the extension of his ego as he strives for advancement. In the process, either partner—or both— may lose the desire to communicate.

As a matter of fact, they do communicate! As one writer put it, "You cannot not communicate." Norman Rockwell's famous painting *At the Breakfast Table* depicts a wife isolated from her husband by the newspaper in which he has buried himself. He is communicating something very forceful to her. There are messages in the slam of a door, the occasional sigh, and the grunt made when someone looks up from the newspaper long enough to answer a question.

Some students of communication have estimated that fifty to a hundred bits of information are exchanged each second. Everything we do in relationship with another is a message. If a wife asks her husband, "What are you thinking?" he may answer with nothing more than a smile and a tender look. This can be more eloquent than speech. The raising of the eyebrows, the frown, the flowers, the kiss—all of these communicate information or an emotion.

Albert Mehrabian presented the results of a decade of communications research in an article in *Psychology Today*. He concluded that words alone account for 7 percent of our communication. Tone of voice and inflection account for 38 percent. Facial expression, posture, and gestures convey 55 percent of communication.

When marriages get into trouble over the lack of communication, it is because the messages ceased to get through long ago. Initially there was only the slightest hint that something was wrong. But the first misunderstanding led to another until the entire relationship became disturbed. If the couple wants to restore their relationship, they need to rediscover how communication takes place.

The Art of Communication

Learning to communicate again may be a bit like taking apart a complicated electrical appliance after it has gone "on the fritz" to see what made it work in the first

place. Just as we may discover that the problem in a
large appliance began with the malfunction of a very
small part, we need to take time in our marriages to see
how our relationships work. The problems may not be
major at all. Even if we have not observed a communication breakdown, a little "fine tuning" may not hurt.

The process of communication appears always to involve three things: the sender, the message, and the receiver. The sender and the receiver may be very different persons. They came from varied backgrounds, had
unique experiences, grew up in diverse surroundings.
All this colors the actual message.

We often merely assume that other people hear our
messages precisely as we intend them. But when
another person reads a different meaning into our message because of background, past experiences, or present
feelings, the message that is received is different from
the one that was sent.

Perhaps, for example, a husband grew up in a family
where there was a lot of good-natured teasing. It was
common in his house to make disparaging comments
about the dress or mannerisms of another. Everyone
good-naturedly took this teasing and returned it in kind.
But his wife has had no prior experience with such
bantering. She receives his good-natured comments as
mean-spirited criticism. When he says, "Are you really
going to wear that?" she takes him seriously. Their differences in background have created the communication
failure.

This might not be so serious if it were not for the fact
that one communication breakdown may upset the entire system of messages exchanged between a husband
and wife. If one does not receive the message as it was
intended, he or she will react on the basis of what was
received. If the wife takes what was intended as a joke
very seriously, she may respond with the slam of a door,
deadly silence, or an unkind retort to the message which

she actually received. A vicious cycle of misunderstandings can begin with one rather innocent failure of communication. What we need for harmony is to make tuning adjustments in the art of communication.

Learning to Communicate Well

Since I believe that communication is an art that can be learned, I am going to offer four suggestions that may help in the effort to communicate more effectively.

First, be sure that your message is clearly received. Especially be sure that your verbal communication reflects your nonverbal language. Some people are masters of sending a double message. Their words say one thing, but their expression or gestures say another. When we say, "That was quite a performance," or "What an outfit!" the listener may not be sure of what we mean. Of course, if we are asked, "Did you mean . . . ?" we can always say, "No, I did not mean that." But if you wish to communicate with your spouse, be sure that what you say is clear in the first place.

Second, communication is not a monologue; it is an exchange of messages. Relationships break down when one party is the perpetual talker and the other usually just listens.

John Drakeford tells how he learned something about communication when he visited a ham-radio operator who had established contact with Drakeford's boyhood friend in Australia. Drakeford was thrilled to hear the voice of his friend some ten thousand miles away. Then he discovered that there were no opportunities for interruption with a ham radio. When his friend had finished talking, he turned the radio channel over, and only then could Drakeford speak. Conversation was possible only when each of them "signed off" to the other.

There must come a time when we, like the ham-radio operator, say, "over to you." Jay Kesler in *Parents &*

Teenagers tells of a teen who once said, "I'm a comma."
When someone asked what he meant, he explained,
"Whenever I talk to my dad, he stops talking and makes
a comma. Then when I stop talking, he starts right up
again as if I didn't say anything. I'm just a comma in the
middle of his speeches." Communication involves a real
exchange of messages. No one person should dominate
the process.

Third, learn to listen. This may be the hardest of all.
Listening is quite different from hearing. We are bombarded by messages all day long. We hear the chatter of
the radio announcer, the background noises of the television in the other room, and the children playing in the
street. But the background noises we hear are not what
we are actually listening to. One problem in communication occurs when the person or thing we should be
tuning in becomes only background noise, while our
real attention is on something else.

Most of us do a lot of "fake" listening. We act as if we
are listening, but our thoughts are elsewhere. Then the
best response is to stop the other person for a moment
and let him or her know that something is breaking
your concentration. Correct the situation and then give
the person your full attention. This shows that you
want to be a responsive listener. Be sure to listen with
your eyes as well as with your ears. To look at another
person who is speaking shows respect and interest. It
also encourages the other person to be open. Concentration by looking also helps us to catch the nonverbal
cues of body language and facial expression.

Failure to listen hurts because it communicates that
others are not really important as persons. Nothing
quite destroys self-respect like the feeling that no one
hears what we say. Developing the skill and concern to
give the other person at least temporary priority over all
considerations can do wonders for the happiness of the
family.

Fourth, communication cannot take place until we get rid of distractions to the process. The television set is on in the average American home forty-three hours and fifty-two minutes each week—an average of about seven hours per day. Has this modern marvel of communication taken away the quality time for family conversation?

Someone has suggested that the best way to discover the health of a family is to notice what happens at mealtime. Is it a time when everyone will be present? Has it been reserved for family conversation and free from everyday distractions? Strong families must insist on reserving a time to share experiences.

The major distinguishing characteristic of a cohesive family unit is that its members *work* at being a strong family. Some potentially healthy families have fallen into bad habits that have allowed the individuals to drift apart. We can rebuild family closeness if we will work to restore the art of communication. The Bible says this in so many ways, including "and be kind to one another, tenderhearted, forgiving one another . . . " (Eph. 4:32).

3

Time for a Family Checkup?

A few years ago the Academy Award movie, *Ordinary People*, described the disintegration of Calvin Jarrett and his upper-middle-class family in a Chicago suburb. One son had died in a drowning incident. Conrad, his younger brother, underwent a four months' stay in a mental hospital following attempted suicide. The father and mother grasped for everything they could to keep from going under.

The fading voices of the church choir suggested in the movie that the answers would not be found in their religious values. The mother's solution to the problem was, "Oh, let's go to London for Christmas. It'll be just like a Dickens novel." The moviemakers seemed to want us to believe that the Jarrett family's breakdown was the natural result of the empty spiritual and monetary values of our culture. Their message was that the American family is on the verge of disaster.

Yet there is a rising chorus of voices telling us that

the American family is not beyond hope. Sociologist Theodore Caplow of the University of Virginia observes that while many Americans think the family is about to collapse, this whole idea is largely a myth fostered by the media. Repeated surveys show that Americans have more, not less, solid relationships with family members than a generation ago.

How healthy are our families? Medical checkups are recommended today for good physical health. What if your family went in for a checkup? How would you do? What would be some of the tests the experts would run?

Why a Checkup Is Needed

I know intellectually that a physical checkup is a good thing, and I go away feeling very satisfied when I am told that I am in good health. But I face those appointments with a bit of dread. I don't really like the idea of asking the doctor to look for something wrong with me!

We may feel the same way about undertaking a family checkup. A well-known political figure said to some reformers, "If it ain't broke, don't fix it." What he meant was that things that seem to work well should be left alone. We may feel this way about marriage. Why get a checkup when everything seems to be fine? There are several very good reasons.

First, things might not be going as well as we think. I have known married people who were totally surprised to discover that their mates were not at all happy. By the time they discovered something was wrong, it was too late. In Leo Tolstoy's novel *Anna Karenin*, Anna became involved in an affair that ultimately destroyed her marriage. What her husband, a great statesman, did not know was that the marriage had failed long before that.

Long before Anna was tempted to be unfaithful, she

felt starved for affection and respect. Although she
wanted nothing more than to be treated as a person, she
never had the opportunity to express her feelings when
things first began to go badly. If her husband, Alexis
Karenin, had only been told what was wrong, he might
have changed his behavior. He learned only after he had
lived in ignorance of his failures for many years.

How many relationships are destroyed in this same
way? All marriages begin with happiness and the promise that the two will always love each other just as
they do on their wedding day. But many things happen.
A young husband goes off to a workplace where his day
is filled with excitement and challenge. He often comes
home to a wife who may have seen nothing but the
inside of the house and talked with no one above the age
of two. If she is fatigued and irritable, he does not understand. Communication breaks down. They live in such
different worlds. The situation could be reversed if only
they took the time to understand each other.

Second, as William J. Lederer and Don D. Jackson
suggest in *Mirages of Marriage*, there is a tendency in
marriage for a movement in one direction to increase
geometrically as time passes. Spouses who are drifting
apart because of annoying little habits begin to blame
each other for the creeping separation. As time passes,
the tendency increases and becomes more difficult to
reverse.

Third, a family checkup is in order because there is
always the opportunity to make good relationships even
better. If your family is happy, you may still discover
something about yourself that will make for improve-
ment. If accomplished athletes and artists still spend
hours improving their skills, it is certainly possible that
the best marriages can be further strengthened.

Fourth, even if your family is strong, there are predict-
able crises in almost all families. Sonya Rhodes and Jos-
leen Wilson in *Surviving Family Life* explore "seven

crises of living together." These include early marital adjustments, the birth of children, changes as children enter adolescence and later leave home, and caring for three generations under one roof. With preventive care, these challenges can become opportunities for growth.

Fifth, the family needs a periodic checkup because relationships are never static. We either grow together or we grow apart. A marriage may reach its full potential at the very beginning and then begin to decline. Or it may grow constantly through the years. When Jesus said, "What therefore God has joined together, let no man put asunder" (Matt. 19:6), he indicated that it is up to us to complete what God has begun.

How to Do Your Checkup

There are many ways to have a family checkup. Some people join with other couples in marriage-enrichment seminars. Others seek out a professional counselor and ask his or her help in diagnosing their marriage. I am going to suggest a method which you can try in your own home.

William Lederer in *Marital Choices* asks couples to make an inventory of their relationship by evaluating the six areas he considers most vital in every marriage. Couples are asked to evaluate their commitment to the marriage, their communication, their "cherishing behaviors" toward one another, how the work load at home is divided, how decisions are made, and how conflicts are resolved. I am going to propose six questions that I believe will help you evaluate the health of your family.

1. *Does your family have a central value system?* Long before our society began to build marriages on the insecure foundation of romance, there were stable marital relationships. When the Book of Genesis describes marriage as leaving father and mother, cleaving to one's spouse, and two people becoming "one flesh," it points

to an irrevocable act. In a biblically based marriage, each person says, "I am with you, no matter what may happen." Such a marriage proceeds not only from the heart but also from the mind. These promises cannot be made lightly or kept carelessly. This marriage is based on both love and fidelity. And faithfulness depends upon having a central value system.

The Old Testament Book of Proverbs might almost be called a manual on parenting. There are 915 verses in the book, and 209 of them—almost one-fourth—are about rearing children. The book tells parents to warn their children against the dangers of sexual experimentation, violence, drunkenness, bad language, criminal behavior, financial mismanagement, and disrespect for parents. Nearly 3,000 years ago, when Proverbs was written, the importance of having a shared value system was highly significant for healthy family relationships. Strong buildings rest on solid foundations. Healthy families respond to a higher authority.

2. *How well do you communicate?* Marriage goes flat when people do not know how to share their problems and their joys. Paul Tournier has observed that our conversations sometimes become like dialogues of the deaf. Each speaks primarily to set forth his or her own ideas, to justify personal actions, or to accuse others. Few exchanges of viewpoints manifest a real desire to understand the other person.

The movie *Kramer vs. Kramer* focuses on a father and son who are learning to communicate. It becomes obvious that communication is more than just talking. It is sharing one's fears and desires. During the production of the movie, Director Robert Benton realized that he was not communicating with his own son. He would go home and hear the boy talk, but only part of his mind was on his son's concerns.

We know the feeling. Communication is more than spoken words. It is the understanding that occurs when

Dad's eye meets his son's, when Mom picks up on her daughter's downcast look, when two people laugh together over a silly mistake.

3. *Do you affirm and support each family member?* Jane Howard has written, "Call it a clan, call it a network, call it a tribe, call it a family. Whatever you call it, whoever you are, you need one." As Robert Frost put it, "Home is the place where, when you have to go there, / They have to take you in." We all need a place where we are affirmed for who we are, not for our abilities or our achievements, where people like us and we like them—a place of acceptance.

This acceptance involves dealing with failure. I heard of a congregation whose building has orange doors. There is a saying in that church that when you come through the orange doors, it matters not who you are, what you have done, or where you have been—you start life anew. It is their way of saying that its people are accepted and loved and affirmed. The healthy family is like this. Individuals may not approve of actions taken by other family members, but they always accept and love them.

4. *Is your family's work load fairly distributed?* Dolores Curran in *Traits of a Healthy Family* reports that a disproportionate number of oldest daughters in large families do not marry. This is apparently because the firstborn is often given too much responsibility for the behavior of the younger children.

Male and female roles are changing rapidly in our society. About 53 percent of American families have two wage earners. More than one-half of the mothers with children under six are in the work force. Whose job is it to wash the supper dishes or carry out the garbage if both spouses work? Continual self-assertiveness about who-should-do-what will destroy relationships. Deepest intimacy between spouses is not possible apart from a genuine equality, a partnership. Each spouse should give to the other the greatest freedom and encouragement to use his or her full intelligence, creativity, and productive energies.

5. *Are decisions made fairly?* The emphasis on "liberation" in our society is producing both good and bad effects. Feminine liberation is good when it means that women are treated as partners in marriage, but there is a phony type of liberation that may lock two people in competition. Each is afraid the other will get the upper hand. In Christian marriage the husband is the "head of the wife," but wives are "joint heirs of the grace of life" (Eph. 5:23; 1 Peter 3:7). Husband and wife are "subject to one another out of reverence for Christ" (Eph. 5:21).

As relationships deepen, as a family expands and grows, its members must be flexible. Family "rules" are revised as the family changes. New curfews, dress restrictions, and friendship guidelines may emerge as a child matures. Families who value compromise in the areas affected by change, yet remain committed to the unchanging values and vitrues of life, build strong relationships.

6. *Are conflicts resolved promptly?* The difference between the healthy and the unhealthy family is not whether conflict ever occurs. In strong families, conflicts become stages for growth. Whereas in some marriages, the first sign of discord leads to divorce, other couples learn to laugh over their disagreements and resolve their problems together. They "do not let the sun go down" on their anger (Eph. 4:26).

Healthy families respect one another's opinions and preferences without necessarily approving of them. I know of one family where the mother loves country-western music, the father is a classical-music buff, and the teenager listens to Michael Jackson. As a child you may have played in a Davy Crockett coonskin cap, but your four-year-old wants a He-Man belt. Faded blue jeans and recycled army jackets are not too difficult to understand if one remembers bobby socks and Bryl-creem. Genuine concern for one another overcomes these minor differences in style and taste.

Improving Relationships

John M. Drescher in *If I Were Starting My Family Again* tells of being almost asleep one night when his three-year-old son came into the room and stood by his bed. Drescher asked what he wanted. "Nothing, Daddy," he said. "I wanted to crawl in beside you and talk a little." Drescher pulled back the covers and his son crawled in.

There was a short silence and then his son said, "Daddy, it was fun holding your hand in front of that lion's cage." The father agreed and asked if he was afraid.

"Just a little bit." There was another pause, and then the three-year-old said, "We really had a good time together today, didn't we, Daddy?" The father replied, "We sure did."

Then the little guy threw back the covers and went quickly to his own room and to bed. He was soon sound asleep. Drescher later wrote, "But I remained awake for some time. My small son awakened me anew to the importance of taking time to be together as a family."

Relationships. These are what healthy families are all about.

4

How to Discuss God in Your Home

Little Johnny looked up from his long line of Matchbox cars and asked his mother, "Who made God?" She replied, "Nobody made God. He has always been alive."

Johnny decided to press the issue: "How did God get born?" His mother knew there was no satisfactory answer to his question. Finally she said, "God is different from people. He did not have to be born." Johnny seemed satisfied, but his mother wondered how a parent is supposed to explain God to a four-year-old mind.

Early in Mark Twain's *Huckleberry Finn*, Miss Watson was encouraging Huck to pray. Huck said, "She told me to pray every day, and whatever I asked for I would get it. But it warn't so. I tried it. Once I got a fish-line but no hooks. It warn't any good to me without hooks. I tried for the hooks three or four times, but somehow I couldn't make it work."

Finally, after more thinking about the subject of prayer, Huck concluded, "No, says I to myself, there ain't nothing in it."

Whether it is our small child's desire to know where God came from, or our teenager's wrestling with the effectiveness of prayer, we struggle as parents with how to teach spiritual principles to our children.

Influencing Our Child

Experts tell us that two things happen when we teach a child. First, the child remembers some of the facts. Second, the child forms new attitudes and beliefs. Johnny may only remember some of the facts about God's origin, but his mother's answer makes a permanent impact on his attitudes and beliefs about God.

In *Dr. Dobson Answers Your Questions*, psychologist James Dobson suggests that the most significant learning period in a child's life is around age five or six. Until that age, a child believes in God only because the parents say so. At five or six he or she begins to adopt or reject various viewpoints. This is a crucial period for discussing God in the home.

Another pivotal period in the child's spiritual development comes during the freedom-seeking teen years. Some teens resent being told what to believe. They talk of having religion "jammed down their throats."

John Westerhoff suggests in *Will Our Children Have Faith?* that a child goes through four levels of faith. Initially there is the *experimental* level, when the child becomes aware of spiritual principles through other individuals. A second level is reached when a child begins to sense some *belonging* to the spiritual family. The third level involves *searching*, a time when the child begins to question and test the parents' beliefs. Finally the child reaches his or her own faith and accepts God for more *mature* reasons.

Toward a Mature Faith

How do we help the child move toward a mature pattern of faith? The Bible offers direction at this point. Two suggestions come from an Old Testament paragraph in Deuteronomy. After commanding the people to love God with all their hearts, souls, and might, Moses said, "And these words which I command you this day shall be upon your heart; and you shall teach them diligently to your children, and shall talk of them when you sit in your house, and when you walk by the way, and when you lie down, and when you rise" (Deut. 6:6, 7). This paragraph suggests two basic ways of instilling religious faith.

First, the parent must fully accept the faith. Children watch parents carefully. They imitate behavior, but notice any inconsistencies. They learn what the parent really believes by comparing what the parent does with what the parent says.

Medical doctor Annette Hollander affirms in *How to Help Your Child Have a Spiritual Life* that visual lessons impress children more than verbal teachings. If a parent loves, respects, shows compassion, exhibits wisdom, and deals effectively with negative circumstances, the child is likely to follow that example.

Children have an uncanny knack for separating the real from the counterfeit. Margery Williams Bianco's *The Velveteen Rabbit*, a child's book, has a dialogue between the old skin horse (around the nursery awhile) and a new toy rabbit. The rabbit wants to know what it means to be real. The old horse replies: "Real isn't how you are made. It's a thing that happens to you. When a child loves you for a long, long time, not just to play with, but *really* loves you, then you become *Real*."

This nursery story illustrates the process of sorting out things that all youngsters go through—rejecting the ten stuffed animals for the one old favorite, putting aside a new doll for the one with hair falling out of its plastic head. The first thing parents must do to instill religious faith is to have it themselves.

Second, children learn about spiritual things from parents who talk of God throughout the day. Attitudes and beliefs are not imparted merely through a brief bedtime prayer or study time. God must surface in casual conversation. He must be pointed out in the sunset. He must be near when a pet dies. In short, he must be part of daily life.

John M. Drescher has written in *If I Were Starting My Family Again* that if he had it to do over, he would seek to share God more intimately with his children. He writes:

> I would notice with my child how God, for a half hour each day at sundown, paints and frames a new picture with the beautiful colors he chooses. . . . I would take time to notice how, in the evening moisture, God makes each leaf look like it has been dipped in the icy liquid of greenness. I would notice, with my child, how God lights the sky with the stars and how he visibly recreates the world during the darkness, making all creation ready for each new day. . . .
>
> Then we would look at the lichen-painted rocks and we would listen to the song of our Father's birds. . . . I would seek more time to stroll by some stream, to pick my Father's flowers, and to see the great Creator in the small as well as the great things of his creation. . . . I would find more time to take sleeping bags in the summer and lie, with my family beside me, under God's heaven and speak of the stars, listen to the noises of nature, the wind whispering in the trees, and the small sounds of unseen creatures. I would provide my child with shelves and drawers on which he could place his trophies and collections.

A parent who believes God is everywhere at every moment will be able to use any place at any time to talk about God.

In addition, a New Testament paragraph that offers direction on how to discuss God in the home is found in Ephesians: "Fathers, do not provoke your children to anger, but bring them up in the discipline and instruction of the Lord" (6:4). Two aspects of teaching about the Lord are suggested: *discipline*, or action; and *instruction*, or words.

Discipline has received a great deal of bad press recently. The kind of parental discipline discussed in Ephesians is at the opposite end of the spectrum from what the media calls child abuse. Discipline should not be equated with the paddle. Discipline is action that encourages the child to listen to teaching. In the Old Testament Book of Proverbs, children are told fifty-one times to listen to their parents.

Ephesians also instructs fathers to tell their children about God. Proverbs stresses the father's role in passing on the family's faith to the offspring. The phrases "Hear, my son" and "your father's instruction" are liberally scattered throughout the parenting sections of the book.

The preceding four directives seem simple. We are to believe what we teach, make God part of everyday life, discipline to provide a structure for learning, and give children direct instruction. But do these directives work? How can we ensure their success?

Reinforcing Our Teaching

Teaching children about God differs from telling them how to turn on the computer and put in the floppy disk, how to set the table for company, or how to tie their shoes. What we ultimately want to communicate about God is far more than facts. We want to share his characteristics—his love, his forgiveness, his concern, and his deep desire to be friends with us. It is one thing to talk about love; it is quite another to give and receive love. We can give our children information about friendship, but this is different from actually having a friend.

Parents teach their children about God most effectively when they provide opportunities to experience God's qualities. When the child feels accepted by a father who is himself accepted by God, when the child knows forgiveness from a mother who herself has received forgiveness from God, when the child senses his parents' concern as originating in the heart of God—then the child comes to know God in a way beyond facts.

How can you know if you are leading your children to know the real character of God? Five questions may help you to evaluate the effectiveness of your teaching. Ask yourself the following:

"Do I have a positive relationship with my child?" Positive feelings toward parents provide a hospitable environment for teaching about God. The loving warmth of a strong parent-child relationship offers greater hope for communicating God's love than any eloquence of verbal expression.

"Do I help my child see the connection between what one says and what one does?" There must be a link between what we say and how we act. The parent who claims to love God must allow that belief in God to show through in responses to other family members.

"Do I teach my children at their own level?" A two-year-old cannot read or write, but can benefit from holding a pencil and looking at the giant letters in a nursery book. The toddler cannot totally understand the concept of God, but we can begin to speak of God to him or her in a meaningful way. Children, especially the very young, have short attention spans. Brevity is important. A good rule is to allow the child's questions to guide the direction and level of the learning situation.

"Do I make the learning enjoyable?" One Sunday-school teacher was stressing the importance of the Ten Commandments to her restless six-year-old class when she decided to ask them to make a list of their own. One young lad immediately suggested, "Thou shalt have fun." His suggestion will never make the official list, but he knew that he wanted to enjoy what he was doing. Pleasant words, smiles, honest praise, and laughter combine to make learning about God enjoyable for children.

"Does my teaching involve repetition?" When children enjoy an activity, they always say, "Let's do it again. Please!" A child with an interest in water wants to hear the story of Noah repeatedly. Another may ask again and again to sing a happy song about God's love. If you use some imagination, what becomes wearying repetition for adults may be an exciting time of learning for the young.

The Ultimate Test of Faith

There was a story in the news a couple of years ago about George Jaeger, his three sons and his elderly father, who had gone fishing on the Atlantic Ocean. A dead engine, a sudden storm, and growing darkness put them in serious trouble. Finally they tightened their life jackets, roped themselves together, and slipped into the black water. One son swallowed too much water and drowned. Then the other two. Then the grandfather. Only George made it to shore. He later recalled that before his youngest son slipped below the surface of the water, he had called to his father and said, "I'd rather be with Jesus than go on fighting."

This is a tragic story of the ultimate test that may come to any family. This son had learned well about God. He kept his faith to the very end. This is the hope we all have—that our children will keep their faith, which we work so hard to instill, to the very end.

5

How Does A Family Define Success?

Early in the nineteenth century, a Frenchman named Alexis de Tocqueville traveled in this country for a year and wrote his observations about the American people. Some of his remarks sound as if they were written today. For example, he said in his book *Democracy in America*, "No Americans are devoid of a yearning desire to rise, but hardly any appear to entertain hopes of great magnitude or to pursue very lofty aims. . . . They care much more for success than for fame."

Tocqueville thought that Americans had an unusual, excessive love for success. A century and a half later, our television commercials seem to confirm his opinion. We do not want to be left in the pack with everyone else. We dream of success for ourselves and our loved ones.

Defining Success

Americans have a custom at Christmastime that is peculiarly our own. We often use the occasion to write a Christmas letter to old friends who are separated from us. Rather than send a Christmas card, we send a photocopied letter that is full of news about the entire family. These letters may be one way to find out what we value most highly for our families.

What do we tell the friends we have not seen in years? The letter usually goes something like this: John and Mary write about the most spectacular events in their lives. John has been made president of his company, the youngest president in his company's history. Mary has been elected president of the Junior League and is busy with the demands on her schedule. And the children? Johnny will graduate with honors from his high school and now must make the difficult choice between the colleges which are actively recruiting him and offering academic and athletic scholarships. Little Susan sings beautifully, is at the top of her class, and was chosen head cheerleader. The whole family is apparently bringing home one trophy after another for their outstanding achievements. They are obviously "successful."

I have exaggerated a bit, but these letters indicate what we generally consider to be a successful family. The individuals are competing in their respective fields and rising to the top. Is there room in the achievement-oriented family for the child who does not excel? Or the father who fails in his business? Or the mother who cannot handle being a leader in community organizations?

We all want success for ourselves and our families. But what *is* success? One family is frustrated because no member reaches the head of the class or becomes an officer of the company. Another family writes those glowing Christmas letters, full of achievements and honors, but something is still missing in their home life.

The problem comes in the way success is defined and in the goals for which we are aiming. Joseph Epstein has discussed the meaning of success in *Ambition: The Secret Passion*. To the ancient Greeks, success was living up to the ideals of good citizenship. During the Middle Ages, success was defined in terms of serving God. Today's success is often equated with wealth, power, and prestige.

Epstein says that we Americans have gotten caught up in a cruel hunger to "make it." He says that until recently a man in Italy or France might have been perfectly satisfied to be a waiter. A son might have been happy to follow in his father's calling. But not in America. Here a man works hard as a waiter precisely because he has hopes for his son to advance beyond his own place in life.

America is a nation of tremendous wealth and great opportunity. We believe in progress and upward mobility. Our slogans announce that anyone can reach the top, regardless of his or her origins. Although this is partially true, it places enormous strains on individuals to prove themselves.

There is always a higher level of status to be attained: a classier make of automobile, a house in a more exclusive township, a more expensive suit of clothes, or a more prestigious school for our children. We must evaluate just how important these goals are in the broader context of daily living.

The Craving for Success

I have two objections to this craving for success. First, although we all like nice things—shiny cars, pretty homes, exciting vacations—there is something absurd about making these things ends in themselves. In Tocqueville's report on America, he wrestled with the way to control personal ambition and keep it in proportion without entirely starving its motivating force. Then he added that he believed democratic societies have much less to fear from overambition than from "the mediocrity of desires."

Instead of "mediocre desires," we might have substituted "trivial pursuits." Are our goals in life trivial? There are many examples of those who have used their financial success for larger aims. I think of the universities and medical-research facilities that bear the names of Rockefeller, Carnegie, and other financial giants. There must be goals greater than the wealth itself if the word *success* is to be meaningful.

Second, an inordinate craving for success breeds failure in human relationships. Some of the greatest novels and movies have depicted the misery of so-called successful people. *Citizen Kane* was a classic film about one of America's publishing giants. When he made it to the top, he discovered nothing but misery in his relationships with others. Successful people sometimes have very unsuccessful families. J. Paul Getty, founder of an oil empire, said, "I hate and regret the failure of my marriages. I would gladly give all my millions for just one lasting marital success."

It is possible, of course, to have a successful family and material success as well. But if we have only "trivial pursuits," our possessions will own us. John Ruskin told of a man who tried to swim from a wrecked ship. He tied around his waist a belt with two hundred pounds in gold attached, because he could not bring himself to leave it behind. He sank and drowned. Ruskin asked, "As he was sinking, had he the gold, or had the gold him?"

The only success worth having is deeper than the achievement of power, wealth, and prestige. William James, the Harvard psychologist, once asked, "What makes a life significant?" He answered that significant persons "worked and endured in obedience to some inner ideal. . . ." Success, I believe, involves reaching a goal that is worth reaching.

A Different Kind of Success

I doubt if many of us are fooled when we receive the computerized mailing that says, "Congratulations! You are a finalist to win one hundred thousand dollars." You have seen advertisements for those seminars that tell you how to become rich. And there are the books whose authors promise to "see you at the top" or tell you "how to think and grow rich." We Americans buy an amazing amount of materials in our quest to become successful.

Many of the success books tell us how to get on in the world by manipulating people. Dale Carnegie's famous book, *How to Win Friends and Influence People,* sold millions of copies in the height of the depression. Although it contains many helpful bits of advice, it also implies that success is measured by the trip up the ladder and that you get to the top by getting others to do what you want. Isn't there more than this to life—both for the individual and for the family?

As a Christian, I cannot forget that my faith began with the One who had "nowhere to lay his head" (Luke 9:58). His story began in a manger and ended on a cross as people were hurling words of abuse at him. Even Jesus' followers were disappointed as they left Golgotha that day. Was his life a success?

I think also of a man named Paul, who knew what it meant to be hungry, sleepless, and anxiety-ridden. He brought these problems on himself when he chose to give up a list of promising achievements in order to become a Christian.

Paul tells about the achievements and his decision: ". . . If any other man thinks he has reason for confidence in the flesh, I have more: circumcised on the eighth day, of the people of Israel, of the tribe of Benja-

min, a Hebrew born of Hebrews. . . . But whatever gain I
had, I counted as loss for the sake of Christ. Indeed I
count everything as loss because of the surpassing worth
of knowing Christ Jesus my Lord. For his sake I have
suffered the loss of all things, and count them as refuse,
in order that I may gain Christ" (Phil. 3:4–8). Was Paul
a success? He had thrown away mediocre desires for
higher goals.

We never seem to be satisfied with the end results of
our "trivial pursuits." But Paul could write from prison,
"Not that I complain of want; for I have learned, in
whatever state I am, to be content. I know how to be
abased, and I know how to abound; in any and all circumstances I have learned the secret of facing plenty
and hunger, abundance and want. I can do all things in
him who strengthens me" (Phil. 4:11–13).

The Successful Family

If success involves reaching a worthwhile goal, Paul
was on his way to success, though in prison. And if
today's successful individual is someone who has discovered a goal that is worthwhile, a successful family
must be one in which the whole family is aiming toward such a meaningful goal together. A successful
family is more than a group of super-achievers who happen to live under the same roof. It must be something
more than the family we read about in many of those
Christmas newsletters!

The Letter to the Hebrews describes the church as a
company of pilgrims on the way to their goal in the
Promised Land. There was no question of their having a
worthwhile aim. The writer says they had "joyfully accepted the plundering of their property," since they had
found "a better possession and an abiding one" in Christ
(Heb. 10:32–34).

One feature in this description of the church as God's

pilgrims is that the writer insists that no one could reach the heavenly goal alone. The church was the community where people came together regularly to encourage each other. They did not want any dropouts along the way. The writer heartened them, "Therefore lift your drooping hands and strengthen your weak knees, and make straight paths for your feet, so that what is lame may not be put out of joint but rather be healed" (Heb. 12:12–13). He knew that some would have difficulty finishing the course. Some would become sick or injured. But the people of God stopped long enough to be sure that the weakest members of the church family were not left along the way.

Have the ideas of success become so distorted in some families that there is no place for the straggler and the nonachiever? Some of the most successful families I know are those that have been tested by misfortune. One has a child that is mentally retarded. The mother is in poor health. The father is caught in a dead-end job. None of the other children is a super-achiever. There are not many glowing achievements for them to write about. But they are truly successful, because they care for each other. All the trophies and awards a family might gain cannot replace the care and support a family exercises when one of its members needs help and understanding.

F. Scott Fitzgerald in his classic *The Great Gatsby* wrote about a man who was the most celebrated success story of his day. Gatsby, with his glittering parties and his mansion, was the envy of many people. But he died a ruined man. In the closing lines of the novel, the main character says of Gatsby:

> He had come a long way to this blue lawn, and his dream must have seemed so close that he could hardly fail to grasp it. He did not know that it was already behind him, somewhere back in that vast obscurity be-

yond the city, where the dark fields of the republic rolled
on under the night. . . .
   Gatsby believed in the green light, the orgiastic future
that year by year recedes before us. It eluded us then, but
that's no matter—tomorrow we will run faster, stretch
out our arms farther. . . . And one fine morning—
   So we beat on, boats against the current, borne back
ceaselessly into the past.

Gatsby, despite his wealth, never found the success he
wanted, mainly because he did not find anyone who
really cared for him.

The greatest success, for the individual or for the
family, comes with relationships—human bondings of
mutual care and concern. Robert Louis Stevenson wrote
in "The Meaning of Success":

> That man is a success
> who has lived well, laughed often and loved much,
> who has gained the respect of intelligent men
> and the love of children;
> who has filled his niche
> and accomplished his task;
> who leaves the world better than he found it
> whether by
> a perfect poem
> or a rescued soul;
> who never lacked appreciation of earth's beauty
> or failed to express it;
> who looked for the best in others
> and gave the best he had.

6

What Teenagers Need Most

There is an event in family life that parents can scarcely prepare for, expected though it is. It comes suddenly—so suddenly that we are a bit amazed when it happens in our own family. One day we are enjoying the pleasant company of an elementary-school child. The next day we notice that our son or daughter has taken on the characteristics of adulthood. One moment we are respected companions, the source of authority and wisdom on everything. The next moment we are neither companions nor the source of authority on any of the questions of life. Our teenager has found new companions and authority figures.

We know intellectually that children pass through the stage called puberty, but how do we prepare for this seemingly new person who lives in the room once occupied by our little child? Concerned and conscientious parents search for ways to deal with their teenage children. Should they give them complete freedom or limit

it? Should they pick their teenagers' friends or leave this
to the young people themselves? Behind the many questions parents ask is one fundamental concern: What do
teenagers need most?

Teenage Independence

Almost every culture has its ritual to mark the moment when the child is no longer considered a child.
Among Jewish families, a boy's bar mitzvah has long
been celebrated at the age of thirteen. Sociologists use
"rite of passage" to describe the ceremony when children begin to enter adult life.

Do we have such a "rite of passage" in our culture?
Someone has suggested that it is the moment when the
adolescent receives a driver's license. This license is the
gateway to a new independence. It signifies the freedom
of teenagers to choose their friends, do without their
parents' supervision, and go where they choose.

Movie and television listings indicate that one of the
most frequent themes today involves restless teenagers
who form their own culture where no adults are allowed
to intervene. The common thread running through
many of these films is that the new freedom provided by
the automobile is the opportunity for experimentation
with sex, liquor, and even drugs.

Many of these movies undoubtedly exaggerate the in-
cidence and glamor of these vices in order to provide a
world of lurid fantasy. The films may reflect more the
fantasies of the older generation that makes the movies
than the experiences of most teenagers. But the films
are right about one thing: teenagers have a strange new
world, a closed society. And we parents are shocked to
recognize how little influence we have over its customs.

If we, for example, painstakingly try to introduce our
young to our tastes in music, we discover that the preferences of their friends are far more important to them

in this and most other areas. We even discover that they have ideas of their own about religion and morality. Although we know that decisions must ultimately be theirs, we want them to share our values. There are anxious moments when they spend far more time hearing other voices than our own.

Is there a parent of a teenager who has not agonized over how he or she should relate to this stranger in the house? There is no recipe to follow. Every teenager is different. There is no way to measure precisely how much freedom to give or when to allow adolescents to discover their own way. But there are guidelines which can help us give our children what they need most.

Parents Who Understand

Perhaps the one thing our children need most during the teenage years is our understanding that life is not easy for them during this adjustment period. An exterior of rebellion and independence often masks some very deep insecurities that our teenagers do not or cannot put into words.

On the one hand, they really are still dependent children. On the other hand, they have taken on the physical characteristics of adults. The figure changes in the girls, the change of voice in the boys, the rapid growth that transforms them almost overnight—all these are a shock to them, as they may be to us as parents. They will probably not want to discuss these bodily changes with us, but they are unsure of how to handle them.

Teenagers know also that they live between two worlds—the world of their peers and the world at home. They probably will not come to us asking for security and warmth, but behind that rash exterior may be a frightened child needing encouragement. It helps to recall our own teenage years. We wanted desperately to belong, to be accepted by the right group. We wanted to be free to make our own decisions, but we also wanted the security of having our parents there when we needed them.

As teenagers we had temptations we probably never shared with our parents. But life was not as complicated then as it is now. Our adolescent peers knew what the sexual rules were. We knew the consequences of stepping across the line that divided "good" from "bad." And we were rarely tempted with drugs or alcohol. Our teenagers are struggling with tough choices. What they need most is our understanding.

Since adolescents crave a strong sense of self-esteem and acceptance, there is reason for us to be frightened when we consider the hours they spend outside our supervision. The desperate desire to belong to a peer group can lead to dangerous experimentation with drugs, sex, or even crime.

Herbert Wagemaker in *Parents and Discipline* reports a study by the St. Louis County Office of Youth Programs. They located adolescents who had not used any mind-altering drugs—marijuana, cocaine, downers, uppers, or alcohol—within the preceding year. Nine out of ten of these children felt "close" or "very close" to their parents. Drug users did not feel this way. Nonusers were usually *A* or *B* students and were quite involved in extracurricular activities. Religion was important in the lives of 80 percent of them. Parents tended to check on the whereabouts of eight out of ten nonusers. Nonusers of alcohol and other drugs considered themselves more independent than their classmates.

What the researchers found were students who were well adjusted, busy at school, and did not see the necessity for drinking or using drugs. They had the self-esteem to be different from the crowd. Our children need a secure self-image to say no. The only place they can find that affirming security is in the atmosphere we provide at home. A teenager can find acceptance as a person if he or she has parents who show that they understand the confusions of adolescence.

Integrity in Parenting

Our children need us to model the convictions which mean most to us. During the teenage years, they struggle to discover what they believe. Like Holden Caulfield in J. D. Salinger's *Catcher in the Rye,* they may see a world full of hypocrites. They may discover that adults do not always live by the creeds they announce.

Teenagers may act as if they totally reject those convictions. But they are looking for people whose lives correspond to the words they say. They especially want to see that the priorities of their parents' lives match the priorities of their words. If they see adults modeling their faith, it will make an impression.

Perhaps you remember the words of the Letter of James. Although these words were not spoken only to parents, they are appropriate for the parents of teenagers. "Show me your faith," James wrote (2:18). This involves more than saying the right words. Our children need to see our faith and concern about the life of the church and Jesus' call to discipleship. We will show how much we care in our conversation, in the way we spend our money, and the way we use our time.

Many of us were not brought to Christian faith just because our parents knew the right arguments to win us over. What we noticed were their lives. We saw them allow an evening's entertainment to be interrupted by a tragedy in someone's life. We remember their refusal to allow anything to interfere with their regular attendance in church. We know they made financial sacrifices for the things they believed in. What our children need is a demonstration lesson in our values.

Our children need more than a good example. They also need the discipline of firmly established rules. James

Dobson observes in *Hide or Seek* that it is possible to treat a child with respect, even when punishment is necessary. He believes teenagers will tolerate all sorts of rules as long as they are not made to feel childish or foolish.

Grace and Fred M. Hechinger wrote in *Teen-Age Tyranny* that it is impossible to raise children "without the prerequisite of experience and knowledge, plus the prior mapping out of goals of conduct and targets of achievement." They then concluded something very important about the necessity of rules: "There is a vast difference between the age-old human tendency to try to get away with violation of rules, and the permissive removal of such rules and standards in the first place." Teenagers, they tell us, "will always test the limits to see how far they can go in circumventing them." Teenagers need the security of having rules of conduct, even if they do their best to get around them.

One of the rules of our house was that our children would accompany us to worship services. Church membership makes available to teenagers a positive peer group. Here they can belong without giving in to the pressures that exist at school and elsewhere in the community. The church cannot succeed with children if the family does not do its part, but the church and the family can have a great partnership in introducing the children to a proper environment and moral standards.

Along with rules of conduct, our teenagers need unconditional love. The father in Jesus' story of the prodigal son was willing to take back the son who had embarrassed and disappointed him. Our children also need to know that they can return to us for forgiveness when they have made mistakes.

We may be anxious about the outcome of our children. We may think we are sure to fail. But if we give them what they need—understanding, moral values we exemplify, discipline, and love— we will probably not fail at all. Our influence is much stronger than we think.

7

What to Do When You've "Failed" as a Parent

One of the most popular psychological theories today tells us that a child's inability to cope with life can usually be traced back to some parental failure. This is a sobering, scary thought. Parents are afraid of being too stern or too lenient. Some couples decide the job is too big for them, and they choose not to have children at all.

Many parents feel they have failed if their children have not turned out to be what the parents wanted them to be. They have heeded the words of the Book of Proverbs: "Train up a child in the way he should go, and when he is old he will not depart from it" (Prov. 22:6). Yet their children share neither their faith nor their values. The parents are convinced that it is all their fault.

We All Make Mistakes

John Westerhoff observed in *Bringing Up Children in the Christian Faith* that we have children when we are least prepared emotionally and intellectually to rear them. Most of us become parents when we ourselves have so many needs that it is difficult to meet those of our children. By the time they reach adolescence, we are coping with our own mid-life crisis.

Do you feel guilty over the mistakes you made with your children? We all have made mistakes as parents. Some of them were the errors of youth, when we lacked the wisdom and experience that come with maturity. We were struggling to make a living. Our intentions were good, but there never seemed enough hours in the day to be perfect parents.

With the firstborn, there were also the misjudgments we made because we had never been parents before. We did not know the thin line between strictness and permissiveness and were inept when it came to discussing serious and intimate matters with our offspring. We probably did not understand what was going on as a child grew from one stage to another. An infant came without a book of instructions, and we were scarcely prepared to rear it to maturity.

Being a parent is a matter of making judgment calls every day of your life. Many of these choices are difficult. You are never absolutely sure you have made the right decisions, but can only pray and hope that they are sound.

Our Limits as Parents

I have seen so many parents anguish over their children that I want to speak some words of encouragement to you if you believe you have failed.

First, as much as you may try to be sure that your

children accept your values, you cannot escape the fact that healthy children will go through adolescence, a term coined early in this century from *adolescere,* "to grow up." It is a time when children begin to be—at least outwardly—influenced more by their peers than by us, their parents. It is a rare adolescent child who will choose our music or our kind of entertainment over that of his peers. I do not know any parent who faces these years without anxiety about what has been called the generation gap.

The adolescent will often not allow us to know what is going on in his or her world, but yet may be struggling with serious questions. Teenagers are moving from our understanding of the world to theirs. In order to find a faith and value system of their own, they question and test what has been handed down to them. It is frightening to feel that the child is giving up on faith when he or she first questions its value.

Furthermore, parents do not know when this period of growth will end. I have seen parents who scarcely lost any sleep as their children smoothly made the transition to adulthood. In other instances, adolescence lasts a very long and seemingly tumultuous time. Some of these parents think they are failures, only to discover later that their patience with the children has paid off.

Jesus told the story of a young man who went to his father and said, "Give me the share of property that falls to me" (Luke 15:12). He took his belongings, went to a distant country, and wasted everything in loose living. The father must have regretted the results of the son's independence, but he allowed him to have the freedom to make his own decisions.

We parents can learn much from that father. It must have been difficult to allow the son the freedom to leave and to give him his inheritance early. But eventually children must form their own values, and even make their own mistakes. Their new independence does not mean that we have failed, so long as they have been given proper training in their earlier years.

Second, there are forces in society which are beyond our control in their influence over our children. The Jewish writer Chaim Potok has written several stories about the conflict of young men with their parents. In *The Chosen* and its sequel, *The Promise*, young Danny Saunders grows up in a strict pietistic home in Brooklyn as the son of a rabbi. All of Danny's life he has been told that his destiny is to grow up and succeed his father. The Saunders family has produced rabbis for generations, a heritage brought from Europe and not to be denied.

Danny does not question his destiny until his adolescent years, when he discovers his own academic genius. He sets his mind on going to a great university to become a professor of psychology, although his father opposes a secular education. Danny wants to be a good son, but the time comes when he must break from his father's world. He goes on to become a distinguished professor, but his father remains disappointed in Danny's choice.

Haven't we all had that experience to some degree? Danny had grown up in a new world among influences that his father could not control. In today's society, we are not the only ones responsible for the outcome of our children. We share our successes and our failures with our children's teachers, with the church, and with society at large.

Third, we must ask ourselves if our plans for our children are appropriate or realistic. Sometimes children reject values that are false or phony. Studies have shown, for example, that children who are most likely to be attracted to cults come from middle-class families where they have been surrounded by affluence. They join the cult and turn their backs on their parents' materialistic ambition, which they believe is not worth pursuing.

Other adolescents reject parental plans for them simply because they have neither the ability nor interest in fulfilling them. A young person may tune out *all* parental ideas if, for instance, their wishes for his or her future ignore the talents and desires of the adolescent as an individual.

Dealing with Our Failures

It would be easier if there were a recipe that would not fail in bringing up good children, but there is not. How do you cope with failure?

Jesus' story about the prodigal son who left his father to go and squander his inheritance is one with which most parents can identify. In one way or another, our children leave us. Many children reject everything the parents stand for—their sense of right and wrong, their faith. We can imagine the pain and embarrassment as the father adjusted to the possibility that his son had broken with him forever. How long was the son away? One year? Or two? We know only that the situation looked hopeless.

Then one day the son made a new decision. He chose the affirming freedom of his father's house over the empty freedom he had experienced when he was out being his own man. The curtain of the story goes down with the father's sense of failure turning to joy and celebration. The rebellious son had come home, and the father celebrated with a banquet in his honor.

Jesus' point was that we are all rebellious children, and God is the Father who takes us back. But there was a reality in the story that Jesus probably had seen happen. Children who break with their home frequently come back. Parents who do not sever the relationship entirely may one day have a homecoming celebration. The most important thing to remember is: do not give up! Continue to love your children—even when they have made their break and apparently rejected your values. Your story may yet have a happy ending, too.

A friend of mine was talking to a group of church

leaders recently. These were people who had a special commitment to Christian training for students who attend a state university. When the church leaders began to recall their own years at the university, not one of them claimed to have been a faithful Christian at the time. One mentioned that he had been approaching alcoholism at the age of twenty-one. But a time came when he returned to his earlier values—and his parents never gave up on him.

One of England's best-known preachers told the story of his own period of rebellion. He went away to the university and left behind the religious practices of his home. His friends and his habits were the opposite of what his parents would have wanted. Then an elderly aunt came to see him. Although she saw his new lifestyle in the city, she said to him, "John, I still believe in you." He never forgot her words. He changed his life, completed his education, and became an outstanding preacher.

The father in Jesus' story is a role model for parents. He did not give up on his child. He is also a model in another way: he did not make his love conditional. An ordinary father might have taken back his wayward son only after strict conditions. This father forgave freely. He showed that he loved the prodigal as dearly when he was away as he did when his son was an obedient child.

We make a mistake when we indicate to our children that our love is conditional, based upon their behavior. It is hard to be as loving and considerate to the child who breaks away in rebellion as we are to the child who remains at home and is loyal to our training. But we risk the possibility of alienating our children forever if we love them only when they love us in return and do exactly as we wish.

God, the Perfect Model, repeatedly appears to have failed with his own children. Read the Prophets and you will catch the sadness of the Bridegroom who has loved his bride, apparently in vain and without reciprocation.

You will read of God as the Parent who has given his children everything, only to have them reject all of it. But God goes on loving. He is always there—always prepared to keep talking, ready to greet the rebellious child with forgiveness. He never allows us to doubt his unconditional love.

Paul reflected on God's love: "Why, one will hardly die for a righteous man—though perhaps for a good man one will dare even to die. But God shows his love for us in that while we were yet sinners Christ died for us" (Rom. 5:7, 8). God loves us when we are not lovable. The good parent continues to communicate that love, even when the children have demanded their freedom.

Asking for Forgiveness

Parents who believe they have failed probably fall into two groups. First, there are many who worry that they have failed, but are not really to be "blamed." They did the best they could. Even though they made mistakes, they tried. The apparent failures must be placed in God's hands. What we do not understand we must leave to God. The story is not over yet.

There are other parents who know that they made disastrous mistakes with their children. They had no time for their children, and the years got away before they even tried to know and understand them. Others abandoned their children, and they carry a heavy burden of guilt. When you have wronged your children, there is a time to tell them. There is a place for a fresh start— and it may begin when you ask for forgiveness.

Even if you see only failure as the result of your child-rearing, there is no reason to consider that failure final. The story of the prodigal son ended with a welcome-home party. Such parties still take place today. Failure does not have to be permanent if mutual shortcomings are acknowledged in a spirit of forgiveness and love.

8

Why Do We Hurt
the Ones We Love?

William Stacey and Anson Shupe began *The Family Secret*, a study of domestic violence in America, with some startling statistics. Thirty-nine thousand Americans died in Vietnam between 1967 and 1973. During those same years, more than seventeen thousand Americans died in family violence. Women and children were the principal victims.

Stacey and Shupe concluded that if violence in the home were to be classified as a medical disease, our nation's domestic health would be suffering an epidemic. The most frequent kind of violent crime in this country occurs within the family.

Is this a spreading disease? Or are we simply more conscious of it than ever before? I am not sure, although I have seen enough families to know this: the family can be the most loving, accepting, supportive place in the world. Families can work through incredible trage-

dies. Unfortunately I have also seen families suffer with
domestic hurts and injuries that had accumulated for
years.

The happy families and the unhappy ones all appear
to begin the same way—with wedding vows and plenty
of love and good intentions. What happens to make
some families go wrong? Why do we wind up hurting
the people we love? Is there a remedy?

Violence in the Home

There is a gripping scene in the first book of the Bible
that describes how Jacob spent the loneliest night of his
life (Gen. 32). After twenty years away from his home-
land, Jacob was about to cross the river and return to his
old home. He came back as a wealthy man with a large
family. But on this last night of his return trip, he was
troubled. He recalled vividly why he left home in a
hurry. With the help of his mother, Rebekah, he had
played a dirty trick on his twin brother, Esau, and on his
blind father, Isaac. In fact, the very name *Jacob* meant
"supplanter" or "trickster." He had certainly lived up to
his name.

Isaac, then aged and blind, had decided it was time to
pass on the family blessing to the older child. He had
sent Esau, his firstborn, to the forest to bring back wild
game so a feast could be prepared for the great moment.
Before Esau could return, Jacob tricked his blind father
into thinking he was Esau, the brother who was entitled
to the family blessing.

Esau was crushed. His father had only one blessing to
give. The Bible says:

> When Esau heard the words of his father, he cried out
> with an exceedingly great and bitter cry, and said to his
> father, "Bless me, even me also, O my father!" But he
> said, "Your brother came with guile, and he has taken

away your blessing." Esau said, "Is he not rightly named
Jacob? For he has supplanted me these two times. He
took away my birthright; and behold, now he has taken
away my blessing." ... Esau lifted up his voice and
wept. [Finally we are told,] Now Esau hated Jacob because of the blessing with which his father had blessed
him, and Esau said to himself, "The days of mourning
for my father are approaching; then I will kill my brother
Jacob."

                                         Genesis 27:34–38, 41

That was when Jacob left home. He had reason to be
afraid as he returned, because Esau was waiting for him.
Jacob prayed on that last night before he was to meet his
brother, "Deliver me, I pray thee, from the hand of my
brother, from the hand of Esau, for I fear him, lest he
come and slay us all, the mothers with the children"
(Gen. 32:11). Fortunately, time had healed the wounds.
The next morning Esau embraced Jacob in reconciliation.

But Jacob was not through with violence in his
family. He later received the very hurt he had earlier
dealt to his father and brother. Several years passed.
Jacob's sons brought home a tattered, bloodstained
cloak. It was the beautiful robe Jacob had made for Joseph, the favored firstborn son of Jacob's beloved Rachel.
The jealous brothers told Jacob that Joseph was dead—
killed by a wild animal. The man who had brought grief
to his father and brother now himself had plenty to
grieve about.

Actually Joseph was not dead, but Jacob lived with his
grief for years before he learned that the brothers had
sold Joseph into slavery in Egypt. The rivalry, ill will,
and jealousy between Jacob and Esau had now been
passed on to Jacob's children. Joseph's brothers had
hated him as surely as Esau had once hated Jacob.

Violence in the family—hurting the ones you love—is
there in the early chapters of the Bible. It began when
Cain killed Abel and continued from one generation to

another. Two brothers, Isaac and Ishmael, could not live in the same house. Nor could Jacob and Esau. Nor could Joseph and his brothers.

In the Best of Families

There has always been more than one way to hurt the ones you love. Cain murdered Abel. Jacob tricked Esau. Joseph's brothers sold him as a slave after he had irritated them with his favored status and his dreams of personal greatness. Physical hurt, verbal and psychological abuse—all in the best of families!

I have mentioned these stories from the Bible because we may have a wrong impression when we hear reports of family violence on the nightly news. These stories may seem to imply that only in the really troubled families do people hurt the ones they love. The Bible reminds us that it happens among solid citizens, in families where the faith is alive and being passed on. Moments come when any of us is capable of hurting the ones we love.

In *The Violence Within*, Paul Tournier recalls the exceptional degree of unity he and his wife had achieved in their marriage. But he also admits that there were stormy times in their relationship. He remembers the shame he felt when he realized he had tweaked his son's ears more roughly and more angrily than he should have.

Mark Twain has a scene in *Huckleberry Finn* where Jim is filled with regret because he has slapped his daughter without mercy when she did not respond to him. Only later did he discover that his daughter had gone deaf and thus could not hear him. He knows he will carry that moment with him forever.

We have all made our share of mistakes, I suspect. Abraham, Isaac, and Jacob made theirs also, but their families survived. Some families survive the hurts and stresses; some go on to deeper pains and injuries. What makes the difference?

Trying to Fix Blame

In the year 49 B.C., Julius Caesar was at Ravenna in Northern Italy, the capital of Gaul. He had just experienced stunning victories in the areas that now make up France, Switzerland, and Belgium. Caesar was at odds with Rome and the Senate, and especially with Pompey, who ruled everything south of the Rubicon River. Since Pompey did not trust Julius Caesar, he was determined to keep him on the other side of the Rubicon or to dismiss him entirely. Caesar finally crossed the Rubicon with his troops, knowing that civil war would follow.

Who caused the civil war? If you had asked Pompey and his friends, they would have said that Caesar rebelled against established authority. If you had asked Julius Caesar and his supporters, they would have pictured Pompey as a tyrant who ruled only to enrich himself. Neither side thought it was the aggressor.

Tournier cites this incident to show how difficult it is to spot the villains when we look at history. One might as easily refer to any recent conflict from Vietnam to Afghanistan. Each side acts on its perceptions of what the other side has in mind. Violence erupts when communication breaks off. There comes a moment when the factions decide that it does no good to talk.

A household often suffers from its own civil war. The time comes when we stop negotiating and begin to hurl the most deadly weapons we can find. Sometimes we throw insults and dredge up old memories of past wrongs, causing emotional distress. Other times the pain is physical. Often it is difficult to determine how it all began.

Three Characteristics of Domestic Discord

The best way to defeat a deadly disease is to isolate its cause. Why do we hurt the ones we love? I am going to suggest three characteristics of civil war in the family.

1. *There is often no villain to be found.* It is like the beginning of the conflict between Caesar and Pompey. We hurt the ones we love because we have two very different perspectives. It is usually not that we are mean deliberately. We injure because we do not understand the feelings of that special person.

A father promises his son that he will be at the Little League game on Friday, but doesn't realize how much this means to the child. Then there is a schedule conflict and something has to be sacrificed. It's the Little League game. The son is hurt and erupts with fury, perhaps with destructiveness.

A husband doesn't realize how important those special days are to his wife—the birthday, the anniversary. He is not sentimental; she is. He is not a villain, only thoughtless. But her disappointment is real and may provide the seeds for future conflict.

2. *We hurt the ones we love because of what Tournier calls "the violence within."* Jacob was apparently a good man, but there was an aggressive instinct—a drive to win at all costs. He had a way of turning a loved one into a rival. Perhaps it was the same way with Joseph and his brothers.

Tournier says that our will to control is even greater when we are sure that we are right. We allow no room for compromise. Our cause becomes God's cause. The hurting husband in one of Nathaniel Hawthorne's novels said to his very pious wife, "As a saint you are wonderful. I only wish you had some sin to make you human."

The Bible reminds husbands to "live considerately"

with their wives (1 Peter 3:7). And it warns fathers not to "provoke their children to anger" (Eph. 6:4). Those lines were written in a world where husbands and fathers had absolute power in the household. They were free to humiliate and trample on other members of the family. The Bible is saying that we must take charge of that "violence within."

3. *We hurt loved ones when we feel that we must settle an old score.* If you kept a count, how many injuries could you add up? How many anniversaries not remembered? How many unjust spankings? How many harsh words of criticism? During the one evening that is portrayed in *Who's Afraid of Virginia Woolf?* every family secret and every injury of the past is recalled with bitterness in front of the guests. It was a moment for settling scores. And it poisoned the relationship forever.

Overcoming the Seeds of Violence

How do you stop this process of hurting the ones you love before it erupts into physical violence? Esau stopped it by forgiving Jacob and welcoming him back with open arms. When Joseph's brothers discovered that Joseph had every opportunity to take revenge, they were terrified. Joseph stopped the cycle of injury. He said, "As for you, you meant evil against me; but God meant it for good . . ." (Gen. 50:20). The Bible emphasizes repentance and new beginnings.

The solution to a pattern of hurting one another is twofold: first, recognize that the villain is not necessarily the other person. There are moments when you contributed to the cycle of injury and pain. Recognize that "violence within," and start over. When the injuries are physical, seek professional help to eliminate that problem. Check the phone book for listings of clinics that provide counseling for spouse and child abusers.

Second, learn from Esau and from Joseph that it is your responsibility to allow someone else a new beginning. At some point or other, we are all a bit ashamed of those moments when we hurt the ones we love. But there is a beautiful possibility for a fresh start for those who are willing to say, "I am sorry."

Ask God's help and forgiveness, too. Trust him for strength to make a new start. If you are not a Christian, express your faith in him by submitting to his will in being baptized. In that act, through God's grace and Jesus' sacrifice for you, your old mistakes can be washed away. You can become as fresh and free as a newborn infant. Then begin to live your faith in your home.

9

When the Family Falls Apart

The 1973 television series entitled "An American Family" offered a candid portrayal of the daily life of Mr. and Mrs. Loud and their five children. In the course of the series the parents divorce, and the oldest son discloses his homosexual activity. Yet through it all the Loud family avoids the painful issues and tough encounters. The eighteen-year-old son observes, "You see here seven lonely people trying desperately to love each other—and not succeeding."

Families do not always succeed. In fact, some seem to be succeeding least at the very time when love is needed most. Christopher Lasch has written in *Haven in a Heartless World* that as the business and public sectors grow more savage and warlike, we look for a retreat in private life—especially in the family. He sees the family as "the last refuge of love and decency."

When the Crisis Comes

But what can we do when the family falls apart? When all our hopes for a "haven in a heartless world" are crushed beneath the pain of separation or divorce? There are some steps you can take.

First, face the crisis. In the long run, the world of fantasy and denial is always worse than reality. Refusing to acknowledge what has happened will only complicate the problem. The healthy response is to admit the truth and do what must be done to minimize its ill effects.

Second, feel your hurt. All failure involves loss, and loss always brings grief, which can be delayed, but cannot be avoided. Your feelings are neither right nor wrong, good nor bad. What counts is how you respond to them and manage them. Give yourself permission to feel pain.

Third, talk to someone. Find someone you trust who will care enough to listen. Just talking about it can help more than you imagine.

Fourth, seek help. The writer of Ecclesiastes was correct when he said, "Two are better than one. . . . For if they fall, one will lift up his fellow; but woe to him who is alone when he falls and has not another to lift him up" (Eccles. 4:9, 10). Sometimes professional help is most appropriate and helpful, but whatever the source, two are better than one.

Fifth, accept your limits. One of the hardest realities to face is the awareness that the only person you can control or change is yourself. You cannot control or change another person. You can, however, manage yourself in such a way that others will be influenced to manage themselves differently. Begin where you can do the most—with yourself.

Sixth, keep in touch with your support group. Crisis time is no time to be alone. We all need people, especially when the family unit, which normally serves as our chief support, is in trouble. Maintain contact with friends, neighbors, and church .

We Choose How to Respond

The steps listed above provide a kind of checklist for action. It is all-important to remember that we can make choices—decisions that affect the outcome of our lives and our families. We often cannot control our circumstances, but we must choose how we will respond and what we will become.

Albert Adler tells the true story of two men who happened to bump into each other in a railway station in Austria. One was an alcoholic living from day to day, begging enough money to buy the next bottle of wine. The other inquired as to how such an intelligent-looking person had come to so pitiful an existence.

The alcoholic began to explain that from early in his childhood the cards of life had been stacked against him. "You see," he said, "my mother died when I was a very small boy. And my father was brutal, so much so that he beat me and my brothers and sisters without mercy. Then World War I came and my family got separated permanently. I have never seen a member of my family from that day to this. So, you see I have never really had a chance. If you had been reared as I have, you would be this way too."

The other man responded: "This is all very strange. To be truthful, your circumstances are very, very similar to mine. I, too, lost my mother at a very early age. My father was also brutal and beat me and my brothers and sisters. And the war separated me from my family. Yet I have always felt that I really had no choice but to overcome these circumstances rather than to be overcome by them."

The two men carried on a conversation until they made the stark discovery that they, in fact, were blood brothers. They were parts of a family that had been separated by a mother's death, a father's meanness, and a cruel war. Products of the same circumstances, they had each chosen to respond in a drastically different way.

Psychiatrist Scott Peck began his best-selling book *The Road Less Traveled* by declaring, "Life is difficult." Once we understand and accept this truth, we can move beyond it. If we assume that life is meant to be easy, we may be immobilized by our problems. We must decide whether to complain about our problems or deal with them.

Positive Ways to React

We can make certain positive and constructive choices.

First, we can decide to respond maturely to life. Peck believes that the basic human disorder is the desire to be the playwright instead of an actor in the drama of life. The immature person merely complains when life does not meet his or her expectations and wishes. The mature person tries to confront life's demands. When the family falls apart, you can either insist that circumstances meet your demands or you can act responsibly in the situation that confronts you.

Second, we can also choose to love destructive, rebellious family members with "toughness." James Dobson has written *Love Must Be Tough* specifically for those who have been victimized by disrespectful behavior from marriage partners or other family members. He notes that most victims are likely to respond out of weakness, to try to appease the guilty party. Such a response is really a sign of lack of self-respect, not of genuine love.

In his experience of dealing with spouses whose partners have been unfaithful, Dobson has found that begging, pleading, and blaming oneself are ineffective. We cannot win respect from others when we have no respect for ourselves. Love must be tough: we must love ourselves enough to act with self-respect, and we must love those who mistreat us enough to insist that they act with respect for themselves and for us.

Third, we can choose to forgive. Lewis Smedes suggests in *Forgive & Forget* that forgiving is love's toughest work and biggest risk. When people are unfair to each other and hurt each other, forgiveness offers the possibility to reverse the flow of our private, painful history.

But we must not misunderstand what forgiveness is. Forgiveness is not merely forgetting. In the Old Testament story, Joseph remembered what his brothers did to him, yet he forgave them. You may recall a childhood accident in which you were cut and scarred. Today as you feel that scar, there is no soreness. Likewise, you may remember a wrong someone had done to you, but there is no soreness if you have forgiven the other person. That is the spirit of forgiveness.

Smedes believes forgiving happens in four stages. The first stage is hurt: someone causes us pain and we cannot forget it. The second stage, he says, is hate: we can neither erase the hurtful memory nor wish our enemy well. The third stage is healing: we begin to see the person who has hurt us in a different light. The fourth stage is coming together again: we invite the person who has hurt us back into our lives.

Why should we forgive those who have played a part in destroying our family? Because forgiveness turns us from revenge. Retaliation can never even the score, but will only repeat the vicious cycle of hurt. Forgiveness is the way back to fairness. Jesus taught us that if we choose to be unforgiving, we close the door to the forgiving love of God (Matt. 6:14, 15).

Fourth, we can choose to start over again. Louisa

Fletcher Tarkington began her poem "The Land of Beginning Again":

> I wish that there were some wonderful place
> Called the Land of Beginning Again,
> Where all our mistakes and all our heartaches
> And all of our poor selfish grief
> Could be dropped like a shabby old coat at the door,
> and never be put on again.

All of us face the problem of getting rid of guilt and starting over again. We cannot do this by ourselves. Frederick Buechner explains in *Wishful Thinking:* "It is about as hard to absolve yourself of your own guilt as it is to sit in your own lap." But God loves and forgives us when we cannot love or forgive ourselves. In his presence and by his grace, we really can start over again. He makes a new future possible. Paul wrote, "If any one is in Christ, he is a new creation; the old has passed away, behold, the new has come. All this is from God, who through Christ reconciled us to himself..." (2 Cor. 5:17, 18). Because of God, we can start over again.

Bringing Good from Evil

Finally, we can choose to use our troubles for the benefit of other people. The first book of the Bible tells the story of Joseph and his family. From the day Joseph was born, he was resented by his brothers. A late addition to the family, Joseph enjoyed a special place in his father's heart and received favored treatment. Jacob's gift of a special coat to Joseph and Joseph's habit of dreaming visions in which he ruled over his brothers made them bitter and jealous. They sold him as a slave and watched as he was carried off to Egypt.

In Egypt, Joseph started as a slave, endured years in prison because of false accusations, and rose to the highest position under Pharaoh as head of a grain-storage

program. And who should show up in Egypt with a desperate need for grain but his own brothers!

The tables were turned. They were at his mercy. Instead of using his power to get revenge, Joseph used it to
reunite his family. After putting his brothers through a
series of tests, he revealed himself to them and said,
"And now do not be distressed, or angry with yourselves, because you sold me here; for God sent me before you to preserve life. . . . As for you, you meant evil
against me; but God meant it for good, to bring it about
that many people should be kept alive, as they are today. So do not fear; I will provide for you and your little
ones" . . . (Gen. 45:5, 50:20, 21).

God does not want our families to fall apart. He does
not intend that we be hurt by seeing the caring expression on a loved one's face being changed into one of
resentment. He wants our families to be "havens in a
heartless world."

But when our family fails to be such a sanctuary, and
when we fail as members of that unit, God can and will
take our failures, our hurts, and our brokenness and use
them to bring us to new beginnings, and revitalized
strengths, love, and hope. He can even use us as instru-
ments of his grace, as agents of his reconciling love, so
that other people may be helped when their families fall
apart.

This really can happen. But the choice is up to us.

10

The Family's Lifeblood

Among the many ingredients a good family needs, nothing is more important than encouragement. David Mace, a well-known marriage counselor, once made a study of families in Oklahoma to try to determine whether strong families have a common denominator. He concluded that the members of healthy families like each other and tell each other so. They give each other a sense of personal worth by affirmation and encouragement.

This is a hunger we all have: to be liked, to be loved, to share our affection and our lives. You are not likely to believe in yourself unless someone first believed in you at home. Yet many families seem incapable of offering encouragement to one another.

Tolstoy commented in *Anna Karenin* that "happy families are all alike; every unhappy family is unhappy in its own way." Many well-intentioned families run aground because there is an absence of praise and en-

couragement at home. We need to acquire new habits
that will support our mates and our children.

Affirming Those We Love

There is a line in the Song of Solomon, that great
book of love poetry in the Old Testament, where the
spellbound bridegroom says to his bride, "You are all
fair, my love; there is no flaw in you" (Song of Sol. 4:7).
In this collection of love poems, the young man and
woman seem to live in a world of perfection. She sings
his praises, and he sings hers. They are obviously two
people very much in love with each other. You can read
the Song of Solomon from beginning to end and find no
word of criticism. There is nothing but praise.

There are moments when we, too, are full of praise for
those near and dear to us. A bride and groom can repeat
the words of the Song of Solomon, certain that they are
marrying someone without flaws. With their rose-
colored glasses, tinted by the power of their love, they
can scarcely imagine what happens in many a marriage.

Something very similar happens when our children are
newly born. As we welcome a tiny infant, so perfectly
formed, we imagine infinite potential. Will she be a con-
cert pianist? A nuclear physicist? Will he be a Heisman
Trophy winner? A valedictorian? New parents are absolutely positive that their own child is destined for greatness and will have the opportunities they never had.

There are exciting stories of children who never ceased
believing in themselves because their parents believed in
them so strongly. I recently came across the story of a
modern American poet. Her name is Robb Forman Dew,
and she is the granddaughter of John Crowe Ransom,
another American poet. When she was asked the secret of
her achievement, she answered that her parents and
grandparents always gave her a sense of confidence in her
potential. "They always thought I could do anything I

wanted," she said. Then she added, "This was astounding considering I nearly flunked everything in high school. My father even told me I could be a neurosurgeon, as he was. There was no reason for his belief in me. It was pure loyalty. It was unreasonable, but it was incredibly necessary to my development."

She mentions that her family's loyalty was so strong that she never felt that she had to "belong" when she was in school. She was not afraid of being out of step with her peers—all because her parents gave her confidence in herself.

Dealing with Failure

We would all like our children to remember that we helped them set their sights high and taught them to believe in their potential. But there is a less savory side to our dreams for our children. Parents may determine that their child is a budding genius, only to discover that he or she cannot compete well in school and must work hard even for a mixture of C's and B's.

With sons, the disaster of discovering imperfection often occurs on the athletic field. And it happens very early for many children. While they are small, we dress them in baseball and football uniforms and enroll them in junior leagues. Then we take the joy out of the game with our fantasies. Parents may be deeply disappointed when they realize that no amount of wishing can turn their child into a star athlete. Instead of encouragement and affirmation, a parent may communicate that the child has failed in the only thing that is important.

It happens in marriage, too. There are the encouraging words, "I believe in you. I know that you can do it." Then each partner discovers the flaws. The young groom has difficulty climbing the ladder of success. The bride has imperfections as well. The couple will find much to criticize in each other—if they look for the flaws.

eas in which we are disappointed and critical of
members are often the very ones that are most
trivial. Why is it so important for our children to succeed in athletics or any other particular field? What's in
it for us? Are we trying to discover a glory for ourselves—perhaps one that we missed out on?

Identifying Gifts

The fact may be difficult to accept, but most people
are somewhere close to average in most things they do.
Yet each individual is unique. The great challenge is to
discover the areas in which our own family members
excel and to praise them for their gifts and encourage
their realization. Perhaps they cannot live up to the
dreams we have for them. But our children may have
gifts that even they have not discovered—precisely because we wanted to mold them into our image and plan
their lives. They may have gifts for working with their
hands when we had pictured them as school valedictori-
ans. They may be artistically inclined when we tried to
push them in a different direction entirely.

Alan McGinnis's *The Friendship Factor* quotes this
bit of advice:

> The secret is this: watch to see where a child's innate
> skills or talents lie, then gently . . . lead or coax him or
> her in those areas. It may be difficult for a father who
> was a crack athlete to understand and help a son who
> would rather play chess than football. But chess, not
> football, is what such a boy needs if confidence is to
> grow in him. If he does that one thing well he will come
> to believe that he can do other things well, and he won't
> be afraid to attempt them.

A pediatrician has commented, "The best families I
see are those in which members care enough about each
other to give a sense of support and self-esteem. The

kids know they are worthwhile because the family makes them worthwhile." One teacher said, "What a loss to our society that some kids aren't affirmed at home. How can they recognize their goodness and gifts if their own parents don't?"

Dorthy Corkille Briggs says in *Your Child's Self-Esteem:*

> The process of building the self-image goes this way: a new reflection, a new experience, or a new bit of growth leads to a new success or failure, which in turn leads to *a new or revised statement about the self.* In this fashion, each person's self-concept usually evolves throughout his lifetime.

A supportive family has an amazing influence in this lifelong development.

It is not only children who need to be affirmed. We all need to be appreciated. The great American psychologist William James once said, "The deepest principle of human nature is the craving to be appreciated." There is not likely to be an adult anywhere—from a corporation president to the most unskilled laborer—who has not felt like a failure at one time or another. Not one of us is as gifted as we would have liked to be and most of us have not reached the level we dreamed of achieving. Home is the one place where we can be accepted and affirmed without having to prove ourselves. It is the one retreat, in our competitive society, for the son who has become unemployed or the daughter who failed to be admitted into medical school—and the parent who wonders whether his or her life will have lasting meaning.

Encouragement in the Early Church

If a stranger had walked into an early Christian assembly, he would have encountered a group that looked like one large family. Its members met in homes, in a family-like atmosphere. The visitor would have noticed that they called each other "brother" and "sister" and "beloved." It might have been a surprise to learn that many of these people had been strangers to each other only months before. But now they were aware that Jesus Christ had brought them together into one large family.

One of the most characteristic features of life in the early-church family of believers was that they enjoyed being together. And one of the reasons they came together often was for the purpose of encouragement. Paul wrote to the Corinthians to tell them what should happen every time they congregated for worship: ". . . so that all may learn and all be encouraged" (1 Cor. 14:31). The church family gathered not only to experience God's presence in worship but also to build up one another.

Paul the missionary saw himself as the encourager of his children in the faith. He reminded the Thessalonians what it was like when he was with them: "For you know how, like a father with his children, we exhorted each one of you and encouraged you and charged you to lead a life worthy of God, who calls you into his own kingdom and glory" (1 Thess. 2:11, 12).

The apostle also wrote to his friends. In these letters he regularly said, "I appeal to you. . . ." One could easily translate his words, "I encourage you. . . ." The lifeblood of the church was encouragement. Like a parent, Paul never stopped offering affirming words of hope and inspiration.

Christians were to pass on this encouragement to each other. When some of the Christians in one church began to drop out of the regular assembly, they were urged on: "Not neglecting to meet together . . . but encouraging one another" (Heb. 10:25). Christians got discouraged and some wanted to quit. They needed the support of the group if they were to persevere.

Three Aspects of Encouraging Others

Just as a large family like the church needs encouragement to support its members, our own families depend on encouragement for their healthy survival. In reading the New Testament, I have observed three elements in encouragement that I think will make a difference in any home.

1. *Encouragement is a challenge to achieve.* When we encourage each other, we indicate that we have high expectations of our family members. Paul wrote to the Philippians, "I entreat Euodia and I entreat Syntyche to agree in the Lord" (Phil. 4:2). Paul was apparently disappointed in these two women, and he knew that they could do better. Perhaps they had been quarrelsome. Instead of scolding them, Paul encouraged them. He showed that he expected more.

Many of us have benefited greatly from parents who drew out the very best in us. We might have settled for less than we were capable of in our school work or our ambitions. But someone said to us, "You can do better. I believe in you." Studies have shown a positive correlation between homes with high expectations and high scores on achievement tests.

I love the Broadway musical *Man of La Mancha*. It retells the story of Don Quixote, an incurable optimist. He believed that the deepest truth is not the way things are but rather what those things can become. He related to people as though they were more noble than they appeared on the surface. When he met the woman Aldonza, she was a waitress at a tavern frequented by mule drivers—little more than a common prostitute. But in Don Quixote's eyes, she was the epitome of everything pure and lovely. He called her "Dulcinea" and related to her as only a courtly knight could.

Aldonza ridiculed the old man and spat at him. She

kept telling him how mistaken he was—that she was not a "lady," but a common harlot. Don Quixote would have none of this and continued to relate to the best he saw within her. As the play unfolds, his expectation has a transforming impact on the woman. She gradually becomes the person he saw within her. In the end, she is calling herself "Dulcinea." One aspect of encouragement is the challenge to achieve seemingly "impossible dreams."

2. *Encouragement affirms realistically.* The flip side of this kind of encouragement is that we must challenge others to succeed without placing pressure on them. It is one thing to challenge our loved ones to fulfill their potential, but quite another to burden them with the implication that they must succeed at everything. Where there is real encouragement, we accept the person even when he or she fails to reach a particular goal.

The early Christians supported each other in times of failure: "Brethren, if a man is overtaken in any trespass, you who are spiritual should restore him in a spirit of gentleness. . . . Bear one another's burdens, and so fulfil the law of Christ" (Gal. 6:1, 2). "Therefore confess your sins to one another, and pray for one another, that you may be healed . . ." (James 5:16). There was a place in these church communities for underachievers.

The family at home should also make room for its members who stumble and fall. There is enough pressure at school or at work without adding to it in the family circle. If the child strikes out in an important inning, he needs someone who is mature enough to place it all in perspective in the game of life, not someone to add to his distress.

3. *Encouragement takes place when we demonstrate how we like being together.* The early Christians were told to "exhort one another every day" (Heb. 3:13). They communicated encouragement simply by their fellowship and spending time together. The feeling that our

lives are important can begin when someone thinks enough of us to suggest that we take a vacation together or spend an evening with each other.

It is tempting for a married couple to seek occasions to build their social schedules without their children, and even without each other. But if we continue to shut family members out of our lives, they will one day turn away completely. We will all find greater delight if we demonstrate that we like spending time together, enjoying the warmth of each other's company and sharing our pleasures, feelings, and dreams.

11

The Search for Intimacy

There was a time when it could not be pronounced in polite society—when the word *sex* was either uttered in hushed tones or reserved for salacious magazines and pornographic movies. Now the topic seems to be everywhere.

The subject that was once discussed in guarded language is now part of the school curriculum. Some self-appointed experts have decided that sexual ignorance is so astounding and damaging that it can be removed only with a concentrated effort at sex education by society at large.

With the right motivation and in the proper setting, sex education may be a very good thing. But I have a problem with the kind of education that comes from hundreds of books on the subject. From Alex Comfort's *The Joy of Sex* to most marriage manuals sold to newlyweds, many of these books seem to leave the same faulty impression—that sex can be reduced to mechanics, techniques, and biological details. Some of this information may be helpful; but there will be no "joy" in sexuality as long as its deeper meaning is left out.

God's Gift

There is a story about a Victorian mother who had her last opportunity to discuss the intimate details of marriage with her daughter, who was to be married the next day. The mother advised, "Just try not to think about it. Put your mind on something else and recall the glories of England."

Some people confuse the Victorian view with the Christian view. Sex is thought to be something unpleasant and shameful, even if it is "necessary" in order to have children. In fact, there is a long tradition of people who considered sex—even within marriage—as somehow degrading and even sinful.

The Bible, on the other hand, frankly recognizes that sex is a part of life—a part that God himself created. There is never an indication in the Bible that when God created us as sexual beings, he "failed." Nor does the Bible indicate that the fall of man automatically changed the God-intended sexual desire within marriage into sinful lust.

The Greeks had the word *eros* to describe physical attraction between the sexes. The erotic urge was not shameful in itself. It was the natural and magnetic pull between people of opposite genders. The Bible openly discusses this attraction between the sexes. When Adam first saw Eve, he said, "This at last is bone of my bones and flesh of my flesh; she shall be called Woman, because she was taken out of Man" (Gen. 2:23). What he saw filled him with delight. He was attracted to her.

The Bible leaves no doubt that men and women find pleasure in each other. There is a line in Genesis where the aged Sarah was told that she would have a child.

The words were so unbelievable to her that she laughed. Then she asked, ". . . shall I have pleasure?" (Gen. 18:12). The entire experience of uniting with Abraham to give birth to a child was a happy prospect.

Sexual attraction is one topic of Proverbs 30. The writer says, "Three things are too wonderful for me; four I do not understand: the way of an eagle in the sky, the way of a serpent on a rock, the way of a ship on the high seas, and the way of a man with a maiden" (Prov. 30:18, 19). Of the great mysteries of nature, none was more impressive than the power of sexual attraction.

The Bible has an entire book about the wonders of romance. In this book, two lovers gaze at each other with wonder and delight, without any shame. One lover says to the other, "O that you would kiss me with the kisses of your mouth! For your love is better than wine, your anointing oils are fragrant, your name is oil poured out. . . ." (Song of Sol. 1:2, 3). Each of them admires the visual delights of the body of the other. They long for nothing more than to be alone together and experience love as a power that overwhelms them.

Why would this poem appear in the Bible? Besides its broad allegorical significance, it apparently portrays what sexuality was meant to be—God's gift to enjoy and to use. Two people today, within the covenant of marriage, can and should enjoy the sexual delights that God intended.

Sex That Dehumanizes

But there is more to be said. Sex can be the source of either the greatest delight or the most painful misery. Frederick Buechner has written, "Contrary to Mrs. Grundy, sex is not sin. Contrary to Hugh Hefner, it's not salvation either. Like nitroglycerin, it can be used either to blow up bridges or heal hearts." One can discover the evidence in the Bible or in the daily newspaper. The Bible has stories of people who perverted their sexuality into something that was used to tempt and seduce, but it also has stories of people who used their sexuality to love and to care for another.

Much of the current literature about the "joy of sex" tends to reduce persons to objects. Since human beings are constructed differently from animals, the real joy comes from giving ourselves to another person. If we reduce the other person to an object for mere physical satisfaction, sex quickly becomes boring and unful-filling. Rollo May, the distinguished psychologist, has commented that the new sexual revolution has not brought greater joy.

Jesus said, "You have heard that it was said, 'You shall not commit adultery.' But I say to you that every one who looks at a woman lustfully has already committed adultery with her in his heart" (Matt. 5:27, 28). Jesus was not suggesting that sexual desires were evil. His rebuke was to the person who concentrates his gaze on another and mentally goes to bed with her. He was telling us not to reduce people to the objects of our desires.

Sexuality is God-given, and sex itself is not sinful. But the joy of sex does not come from endless one-night stands in the search for the ultimate experience. Its greatest joy is experienced by two people who are totally committed to one another for life.

Our culture tends to encourage couples to look for joyful sexuality in all the wrong places. Anyone who believes the propaganda that emphasizes physical beauty or the excitement that comes with the pornography and erotic stimuli confronting us daily will miss the joy that comes from caring for another person.

To Know Another

Helmut Thielicke has raised an interesting question in *The Ethics of Sex*. He asks why it is that even the most enlightened and articulate parents have difficulty talking to their children about sex. Thielicke suggests that the task is difficult because we know that some things simply cannot be communicated verbally. We recognize that there is far more to sex than lessons in biology and anatomy. The experience is so personal and profound that it cannot be explained to a third person in words.

It is not because of prudishness that the Bible speaks of sexual intimacy as the experience of "knowing." We are told, "Now Adam knew Eve his wife . . ." (Gen. 4:1). "And Elkanah knew Hannah his wife" and she conceived and bore a son named Samuel (1 Sam. 1:19, 20). In physical intimacy we communicate something of ourselves to another person that no words can express—we truly "know" our partner.

Elizabeth Achtemeier says in *The Committed Marriage* that we have not exhausted the subject of sex when we provide our children with the facts of biology. She thinks that the primary way to communicate worthwhile sexual values is to allow children to recognize that their parents have a joyful love and good conscience in their sexual relationship. When children see their parents show affection to each other in daily living, they trust that the mysteries their parents understand must be good.

What is wrong with engaging in sexual activity before marriage? Sex is a means for two people who share a lifetime together to communicate their whole selves. Only when one experiences the total joy of physical intimacy in this atmosphere of trust will he or she understand that true sexual fulfillment can never be found outside marriage.

Guidelines for Sexual Happiness

Many married people have serious questions about sexuality. I am going to offer four guidelines for a satisfying life of marital intimacy. These have been gleaned from the Bible and from experienced counselors.

First, sexual happiness can come only when two people meet each other as persons, not objects. In 1 Corinthians 7, Paul was writing to new Christians who had apparently asked what their Christian commitment meant for their married life. Was the sexual relationship good? Or was a life without sexual pleasure a higher form of existence?

Paul answered, "For the wife does not rule over her own body, but the husband does; likewise the husband does not rule over his own body, but the wife does. Do not refuse one another except perhaps by agreement for a season, that you may devote yourselves to prayer; but then come together again, lest Satan tempt you through lack of self-control" (1 Cor. 7:4, 5).

Not only was sexual intimacy permissible for married people, according to Paul—it was to be expected! Paul goes on to explain what it really means for two people to be "one flesh." They have joined their lives to such an extent that they do not have final control over their own bodies. Most important in this paragraph is Paul's insistence that the sexual life of the couple is to be worked out mutually. Both are to live for each other. There is no place for selfishness. The greatest happiness comes when we are more interested in bringing joy to another than in gaining satisfaction for ourselves.

Second, never try to measure your happiness by some standard from the media. You are two unique individuals, and your desires and needs are your own. Reading all the available literature would not bring perfection to your relationship. What really matters is the care that you show for each other.

Third, it is important to remember in a culture bombarded with sexual stimuli that sex is not the most important facet of your existence. Many couples are frustrated in their early married years because there are problems in their physical relationship. They have had to learn that not every sexual experience is ecstatic. Sexual intimacy takes time, patience, and understanding to develop. If the couple can relax and discover that this kind of joy involves a process of growing together, they can be happy even when their sexual fulfillment is not complete.

Fourth, sexuality is part of the total relationship of two people. No one can expect to have a satisfying intimate relationship if there has not been caring and consideration in every other aspect of married life. Marital partners who are thoughtless throughout the day cannot expect physical intimacy to occur instantaneously.

There is a line in Tolstoy's *Anna Karenin* where Anna complains about her unhappy marriage. She speaks of the husband who "never once thought I was a live woman, in need of love." Moments of sexual intimacy are meant to communicate the same affection each partner has shown in many other ways—the compliments, the gifts, the caring gestures. We cannot have one without the other. "Showing love" must precede and accompany "making love."

I believe the Christian couple can know the joy of sex with a depth simply unavailable to nonbelievers. In Christ we have been taught to care for one another unselfishly. As two people grow in total intimacy, they communicate a lifetime of caring and mutual commitment.

12

Till Someone Else Do Us Part

They had been married for over twenty years and were the parents of three children. It had generally been a good marriage, but recently she had sensed a little distance in their relationship. This was disturbing, but not alarming since they had gone through such times before. She knew her husband was facing problems at work.

One evening he came home at the usual time, found her in the kitchen, and after an awkward pause said, "I don't know any easy way to do this, but I am moving out of the house. I am just not happy in our marriage. I doubt that I really love you. I want to do what I can for you and the kids after the divorce, but I cannot stay in this relationship."

The wife's stunned attempt at a response was silenced by his terse "I really don't want to talk about it." With that, he left after picking up a few belongings. Despite many years of marriage, this whole conversation was over in less than fifteen minutes.

Shortly afterward he filed for divorce. There was some disagreement and negotiation about property settlement and child care. Within six months the divorce was final, and he had married again—a younger woman with whom he had been having an affair for several months prior to his announcement to his wife. The wife was shattered about the whole situation. There were many months of trauma and depression before she was able to return to any semblance of normality. Several years passed and many counseling sessions were needed before she reached complete equilibrium.

There were 1,170,000 divorces in the United States in the latest year for which statistics are available. Many of these had an extramarital affair as a contributing cause.

The Affair

The traditional marriage ceremony includes the words "Till death do us part." Despite what is said, or even what is intended when the vows are made, many marriages last only until "someone else do us part." Kinsey claimed from his research in the 1950s that one-half of the men and one-fourth of the women he surveyed acknowledged extramarital affairs. No part of society—not even the church—has been safe from this tragedy. Apparently the tremendous emotional attraction of an affair causes some people to violate the most cherished convictions about marriage vows.

Marital unfaithfulness has always been a problem. The earliest book of the Bible tells not only of bigamy and polygamy but of Judah's affair with Tamar and the attempt of Potiphar's wife to seduce Joseph. Virtually every known culture has set some limitations upon extramarital sex relations and has had some means of punishing guilty parties. But marital unfaithfulness in the past did not lead to divorce as frequently as it does today. This is probably due to liberalized divorce laws and to the prevailing attitudes of our culture.

Sexuality is discussed more openly today, and society does not always place a stigma on extramarital affairs. Flirtations go on constantly, initiated by both sexes. The married person seeking outside gratification easily finds opportunities. The individuals in the affair may not intend to rupture their marriage bonds, but so strong an attachment may form that divorce is seen as the only answer.

Use your imagination for a moment. Suppose you are a counselor. You are trying to save the marriage of a person involved in an affair. We will assume that your client is a woman, although we could sketch the same case with a man. She has come to you because she wants to do the right thing in God's eyes. But she desperately wishes to divorce her husband and marry the "other man."

One of the first things you will discover is that your counselee is very emotional about the matter—emotional in the sense that romantic feelings toward her lover overshadow all other considerations. Her feelings are colored by exciting experiences with her lover: the way they met and "fell in love," times when they have shared intimate feelings, special songs and places. She has found a "soul mate" unlike any she has ever known. It is like the first love of high-school days all over again. The thought of giving up this illicit relationship may bring tears and intense pain.

This wife may think she is making cool, rational decisions. In reality her emotions are deceiving her. In later years she will understand that she was really guided only by her temporary feelings, but at the moment she will find ways to make wrong seem right.

As her counselor you will also discover that she feels fulfilled by the new relationship in a way she was not in the old one. She may ask why she should not have this "last chance for happiness." She may speak of the faults of her present husband and may think that she never loved him or that she realized long before that her marriage lacked something. Perhaps her husband does not communicate with her and appears uncaring. Part of what is being said may be true, but part is to salve her feelings of guilt about the overpowering nature of the illicit relationship.

You may also recognize in this counseling session that the lover has the advantage over the spouse. An affair does not involve all of the responsibilities that marriage does. A meeting in a motel room, where all the talk is of love and of each other's immediate feelings, does not involve the pressures of children at home, broken appliances, housework, financial burdens, and all the irritations of daily life between a husband and wife who have stopped working on their romantic relationship.

This imaginary person you have been trying to help may say that when she married she sincerely intended that it would last forever. But she did not know then what would happen to the marriage or that she would later meet the "perfect man." The new relationship is so promising that the earlier vow no longer seems binding. If you ask how she knows that the same thing will not happen again, she may reply that she is sure this union will last. This new relationship is perfect!

Jesus on Divorce

It is important to remember that there is another side to every situation involving human beings. Jesus discussed divorce in four paragraphs which are preserved for us in the Gospels. In Mark 10:11, 12 and Luke 16:18, he taught that there was to be no divorce. In Matthew 5:31, 32 and 19:3–9, he explained that divorce is permissible only in the case of unchastity—that is, adultery. "And I say to you: whoever divorces his wife, except for unchastity, and marries another, commits adultery" (Matt. 19:9). In all four of these instances his basic point was that marriages are to be preserved, not terminated.

We must remember that Jesus spoke the Word of God. What he said came from the wisdom of the Creator himself. His words may not appeal to us at the moment, but they come from the Source who makes our best judgments appear as nothing by comparison. God stands against "throwaway marriages" in which the individuals take lifelong vows so lightly.

There are other things to remember if you are caught in a triangular relationship. The romantic attachment of an affair is, at best, temporary. A husband or wife who divorces a mate to marry another soon discovers that many of the old problems—and some new ones—appear in the new relationship. As responsibilities arise, life becomes dreary or commonplace. There are conflicts to threaten the romance.

Even before the new problems are discovered, there are the horrors of divorce proceedings. There are squabbles over property and children. No one can fully describe all the torments the rejected parties go through. Families are torn apart, and it is often the innocent children who pay the highest price.

Other relationships are broken or damaged also. Previous friends or even other family members may be estranged. Church relationships may be severely injured. In some cases the divorcing parties completely give up on the church.

Underlying it all is the big lie. The first marriage vows are broken. Promises to God, to the spouse, to the families involved, and to society are discarded. And there is no guarantee that the vows in a second marriage will not also turn out to be deceptions.

In later years there will often be tremendous guilt and remorse over what was done. Marriages that develop out of extramarital affairs sometimes fail just because of guilt feelings.

I believe almost any marriage can be saved, even when it is troubled by outside involvements. One of the tragedies of a divorce brought on by an affair is that the couple never really made a genuine effort to rebuild. For those who will persevere, with God's help, the bad times can lay a foundation for a depth of sharing and understanding that may make the marriage stronger than before. This requires forgiveness and patience. It also demands that relations with the outside party be cut off completely. Although it will take time for the emotional wounds to heal, people who give up too soon rob themselves of the possibility of rich and enduring rewards.

Avoiding Danger

But what can be done to prevent a marriage from getting into this kind of trouble? If we know where the dangers lie, we can avoid them.

1. *Remember the kind of person you are.* In the long run, it is the inner character of a person that will say "no" to temptations that would destroy a marriage. This is why your ultimate values and your relationship with God are so important. I believe that Christians have both the view of life and the power they need to maintain a good marriage. If you understand God's will and accept Christ's teaching, you know that everything God asks of us is for our good. To destroy a marriage is to do yourself terrible damage, even though the consequences may not be immediately obvious.

God knows there are problems we cannot handle by ourselves. Through prayer and the indwelling of his Spirit, he gives strength to the weak. What we could not do by ourselves, we can do by calling on God's power and guidance.

2. *Consider the nature of the world around you.* Many of the conclusions commonly accepted in our culture may not be in our best interest or in harmony with God's loving purpose. Sexual promiscuity, which is so much advertised in the media and portrayed in popular

entertainment, is neither normal nor justifiable. Even if "everyone else" you know practices infidelity, that would not be justification for adultery. It takes great moral commitment to stand by your convictions of right and wrong when it seems that few others share them. But this is precisely the courage we must have to preserve our marriages and our homes.

If you allow yourself to fall into the patterns of those around you, you may find yourself involved in what seems to be an innocent flirtation. Suggestive remarks are made. Casual touching becomes more serious. There are meetings for lunch and other times. Conversations become increasingly intimate. Friendship becomes tinged with desire. Thoughts are entertained that lead to tentative suggestions. If these are received favorably, further steps are taken.

If someone questions your relationship with a person other than your spouse, you may reply resentfully that nothing more than friendship is involved. The truth is that a significant number of affairs begin out of such "friendships." Once a person gets into this progressively ensnaring situation, it is most difficult to stop. It is far better to recognize the dangers before reaching the point where it is difficult to back away. When this special relationship with another person develops, it is not uncommon for both parties to begin discussing their respective marriages. One of the most dangerous lines spoken to a person of the opposite sex is, "My husband [or wife] doesn't understand me." This kind of conversation can establish a bond of intimacy between unmarried persons that almost invariably leads to trouble. One often "feels" married to the confidant long before there is illicit sexual intimacy.

Most people want someone with whom they can share their innermost thoughts and know that they will be lovingly accepted. But when that person is someone of the opposite sex who is not your spouse, and there is a potential romantic attraction, you are playing with fire.

3. *Recall the nature of the marriage relationship itself.* It is so easy to take ongoing relationships for granted. It is so easy to stop communicating, to be insensitive or self-centered. Volumes have been written about the many small ways in which a relationship needs to be built and sustained over time.

Marriage takes work! There must be constant effort by both parties to keep the marriage a good and rewarding relationship for each partner. For those who are willing to pay this price, marital love can mature into the most beautiful union humanly possible. Strong marriages do not just happen by accident.

4. *Remember what the word* love *means in connection with marriage.* It certainly includes romance. It also includes affection and friendship. In the long run, however, marital love must be a matter of commitment. Many married people will have some moment in their lives when they will find another person more attractive than the one to whom they are married. The reason they do not abandon their marriage for a new one is because they meant the promise made at the altar. That promise said, in effect, "I commit my life to you. Regardless of what comes, I will honor that promise. In sickness and health, in poverty or wealth, for better or worse, you can count on me to be at your side." We may not be able to keep our immediate feelings under control, but we can reflect on and honor our promises! Truly committed marital partners recognize the enduring nature of their bonding and also do their best not to allow themselves to come into situations where keeping the marriage vow is made harder.

13

How to Love the Empty Nest

When you bring your first child home from the hospital, your life has changed forever. Most of us do not regret this change, but we do have to make some adjustments in our lifestyles. No longer are you likely to be alone with your spouse for an extended period of time. All of the things you have enjoyed doing together now have to take a third party into consideration.

Those quick decisions to eat out and go to the movies, the planned vacation, the crowded schedule—all of these must be evaluated in terms of the needs of this third party. If you are accustomed to the undivided attention of your mate, you may feel that you have lost it forever. It seems as though your marriage will never be the same again.

Some of us are now going through another period of transition. We have lived for half of our lives with children in the house. From the time the oldest child is born until the last child leaves, most people spend twenty to thirty years—long enough to get used to the constant presence and sounds of the children. It requires as much of an adjustment to see the young people leave as it does for them to enter the household. They call it the empty-nest syndrome. It is not as easy as some people think!

Challenges When the Children Leave Home

A friend told me recently that he had looked forward to having an empty nest. He had pictured resuming the carefree life that he and his wife had experienced twenty-five years ago and imagined all the advantages of the empty nest. There would be the freedom to come and go at will and the release from worrying when the children were out late at night. He looked forward to vacations and buying some of the things they had sacrificed while the children were growing up and going to college. The empty-nest period would be like the early-married years—except this time there was more money to spend.

My friend later found, as most of us do, that it is not all that simple. He had to come to terms with this change in his life. He was scarcely home from his youngest daughter's wedding before he recognized how silent the house had become. The music no longer vibrated from the children's rooms. The house was no longer a meeting ground for teenage guests. Then there were all of the memories that filled the house. There was once so much to do, and there now seemed so little. The crowded, busy years seemed difficult at the time, but now he recognized the value of being needed.

Adjustment to an empty nest may be as difficult as any the parents have ever made—as critical as the day they first began their marriage. For some, it is a real crisis in their lives.

It may be difficult to grasp emotionally the meaning

of the biblical statement that "a man leaves his father and his mother" (Gen. 2:24). We grasp it intellectually when we leave our children at college or attend their weddings. But it may be painful, after all these years, to realize that they will never come home again—except as guests. After his youngest daughter's wedding, one father became very busy in building an addition to his house. When he was asked why he would add to a house now emptied of children, he replied that it was for his daughter and her husband. He could only imagine a life that went on in continuity with the last twenty-five years of his own.

In another family, the new grandparents began remodeling the day after their daughter-in-law gave birth to a baby boy. They turned their den into a children's playroom, complete with bunk beds, assuming that there would be another grandchild soon. Even when their son became a father, they could not accept his absence. They could not face a future without his constant presence in their lives.

This is a poignant period of adjustment because we miss the presence of each son or daughter who made so many demands on our time. We miss the conversation, the mealtimes, the things we once did with them as a family unit.

Sometimes the absence of our children robs us of our own identity. Mel Roman and Patricia Raley wrote in *The Indelible Family*:

> When all of the children leave home and the nest is empty, some parents have no idea who they are or what to do with themselves. Their identity, both as individuals and as family members, has been so tied up in mothering and fathering that they are lost. They feel worthless and useless. They feel robbed of their roles and of their children. . . . Although they mourn the loss of their children, they also mourn the loss of themselves. The children will be all right; they have everything to look forward to. The

parents are not sure that they have anything to look forward to.

Sometimes our identity is almost entirely wrapped up with our parental roles. Roman and Raley say that young women learn at a very early age to become mothers and that mothering becomes part of their self-worth. They spend decades polishing the skills of parenting, and later they are placed in forced retirement because these skills are no longer needed.

In the Broadway play *I Do! I Do!* the couple returns from the wedding of their daughter to the sadness of their empty house. When the wife announces her desire for a divorce, her husband understands that the real problem is that his wife has lost her sense of purpose. After spending her life caring for the children, their absence means that she does not know what to live for in the future.

This empty sadness often hits one parent more painfully than the other. Sometimes it hurts the wife most, especially if the husband's life is still wrapped up with his job. He can turn his energies elsewhere, but she has to face this meaninglessness alone. Sometimes it is the other way around, and the husband may feel he has lost his best companion when a child leaves home.

Besides missing the children, there is also the crisis of becoming reacquainted with the one who was there with you before children ever came on the scene. It may sound absurd to talk about becoming reacquainted with your own spouse, who has been at your side through all of the childhood illnesses, the excitement of Little League heroics, graduations, and recitals. Although your mate has shared your worries and your joys, it may be difficult to take up just where you left off thirty years ago.

Gerald Klerman of the Harvard Medical School has said that the departure of grown children often necessitates major changes in the marriage relationship. The children have been part of your communication for years, yet you may have drifted into your own hobbies and interests along the way. Howard and Charlotte Clinebell have written in *The Intimate Marriage* that some couples develop parallel lives, touching at fewer and fewer points. Now they face each other across the breakfast table or spend an evening alone and realize that their relationship has been lacking in communication and intimacy.

Danger and Opportunity

There are always two sides to a crisis. On one hand a crisis spells danger. Since the marriage has come to a turning point, everything could end in disaster. But the other side is that a crisis is an opportunity to meet the challenge and become stronger. If the marriage is healthy, this can be a great time of rediscovering the delights and freedom that many people look forward to for years.

Imagine how much a couple in their middle years have invested in their marriage. Consider the common memories they share, the mutual experiences that have molded them into one being. That shared history, along with a commitment to the future, can provide the resources for deepening the relationship. They have experienced too much together to allow this challenge to destroy their marriage.

Coping with the Empty Nest

Theodor Bovet, a Swiss marriage counselor, has observed, "Marriage is subject to the same law as all living beings; those who are unable to ripen grow old." How do the successful marriages survive the absence of children?

First, both the husband and the wife must be sensitive to the stresses of this particular time in their lives. Because these pressures often hit individuals in different ways, you will not always understand precisely what your mate is going through. The grief may be more long-lived for your spouse than for yourself, or vice versa. One may feel more useless and lonely than does the other. One of the great secrets to meeting the challenge is awareness of what your spouse is feeling. He or she may not articulate what this experience means, but the loss can be real, nevertheless. Your mate may be feeling "old," and may not be sure that there is anything to look forward to. Now it is time to develop sensitivity to what is *not* being said. It is also important to be especially devoted to your mate's needs.

Second, several marriage counselors have suggested the importance of the renewal of romance between spouses during these years. The soft glow of love can push back the darkness and dissolve the shadows. It can replace the fear of aging with the excitement of a new day. Renewed life can be brought to a marriage by thoughtfulness—perhaps by surprising your mate with some tenderness and token of your love. You might ask yourself when you last did something that showed your spouse the truly special place he or she holds in your life. Everyone needs to be appreciated and loved.

Love can be reaffirmed in more than one way—a gesture of affection demonstrating that the attractiveness of a mate has not diminished, an unexpected gift that indicates what your partner means to you, the willingness to spend time that shows you have not become bored with your companion.

Third, do the things you have put off for a long time. Howard and Charlotte Clinebell have spoken of all the energy that went into parenting, now suddenly released for other activities. If you do not use this creative power, the empty-nest syndrome will hit you especially hard. Some of this vigor may flow into grandparenting, but this is usually a minor outlet. Most of the energy is available for new hobbies, joint projects, and community service, much of which can be done as a couple.

Many of the best leaders in philanthropic and educational institutions are people living between the time when their children have left home and retirement. This is the age of maximum energy and the utmost capacity to get involved with the causes they believe in. Instead of sitting at home with feelings of worthlessness, they find new challenges that give the satisfaction of making an important contribution to society and their own well-being.

Finding Resources and Support

Carl Jung has suggested using the second half of life to develop one's inner resources. Preoccupation with the self is a characteristic weakness in adolescents, but a healthy concern for one's self is a necessity in adulthood. Developing a coherent view of life and coming to terms with one's own individuality is essential for total maturity. Many people allow others to decide everything for them for so long that they lose touch with their real selves. One reason more suicides occur on weekends than in the remaining five days of the week combined is that some people break down completely when their lives are not structured by others.

Together a couple may embark upon a quest of listening to their own deepest longings. This may involve participation in a reading group or beginning a joint hobby. Oscar Wilde has observed, "It is tragic how few people ever possess their own souls before they die." The empty nest presents an opportunity for inner growth.

Marriage needs the support of a larger group at this and every other juncture. Perhaps you have had this ex perience when you moved to a new city. Once you have moved in and the bags were unpacked, you realized that there was no one to invite over for dinner. Although you enjoyed the company of your spouse, the two of you sometimes felt lonely, even when together.

Loneliness also sets in when the children are gone. They have kept you so occupied through the years that you did not have time to feel lonely. Now you need to develop a network of outside relationships once more, just as you did in the earlier days of your marriage. Those relationships may be built within your neighborhood or while pursuing your hobby or other interests.

No place offers a better opportunity for building this network than the local church. A congregation is a large family where all ages have a place, where we are challenged to involve our lives with the lives of others in a common cause. Church fellowship allows us to meet people just like ourselves, but it also introduces us to those who have different backgrounds from our own. This mixture is a great enrichment for our lives. And no excitement can match that of a married couple growing together spiritually.

You can find many opportunities to reach out and use your creativity to help others precisely as you have helped your own children. By examining your own interests and capabilities and discovering the resources for developing them in your community, you can learn to love the empty nest and build an even stronger marriage!

14

Is There Hope for Single-Parent Families?

Experts who look for the key to a happy family life agree on one thing: an essential ingredient is having a mother and a father who love each other. Children benefit by growing up in the presence of both a male and a female parental figure. They learn their first lessons in becoming good husbands and wives by seeing role models at home.

Unfortunately, the family that has two parents at home is becoming much less common in our society. The number of children who live in single-parent families tripled in the last twenty years and continues to rise. In the 1970s approximately 20 percent of all children were living in one-parent homes. It is estimated that 45 to 48 percent of all babies born in 1980 (approximately one of every two) will live with only one of their parents before they are eighteen. It is a rapidly changing world.

A recently divorced mother asked, "Do you have any word of hope for me? I know the statistics. You do not have to convince me that children need a father and a mother. But do you think it is possible for me to do this job with some measure of success?"

Dolores Curran says in *Traits of a Healthy Family* that when she began to tabulate her findings, she hoped her studies would show that it made no difference how many parents there were in the family. She explains: "Because single parents seem already to have so much working against them, and because many single-parent families with whom I work seem as healthy as two-parent families, I admit I was hoping to discover that the number of parents in the home didn't matter." The results proved otherwise.

As the harried father discovered in *Kramer vs. Kramer*, it is not easy being mother and father at the same time. Most of us need all the childrearing help we can get. And a co-parent helps us in many ways. We need their judgment and support. We need them when we cannot be two places at once. Most important, every child deserves to have a father and a mother.

Focus on Your Strengths

Statistics never tell the whole story. Just as having two parents in the home does not guarantee a healthy family, single-parent families are not doomed to instability and failure.

I know fathers and mothers who have lost a loved one through death. I have seen the courage of mothers who were abandoned. Despite the loss of income, the extra burden in being both mother and father, and the feeling that they did not belong in a world made for couples, I have seen single parents who refused to believe that they could not have a happy family. They found ways to overcome difficult circumstances.

What is the secret of these homes that are not defeated by the loss and grief of divorce or death? One answer to this question stands out: those families that succeed in being happy refuse to accept the term *broken home* as a description of themselves. Alice Peppler in *Single Again—This Time With Children* tells of a mother's painful experience while filling out a form for one of her children. The form asked, "Is this child a product of a broken home?" "A *broken* home?" asked the mother. She said to herself, "What do you suppose constitutes a broken home in our Lord's eyes? The loss of a parent? Is it not rather the loss of Christ's presence? Can *any* home be broken if the Lord is its head?"

She went on to say, "A broken home is not yours, not anyone's, unless you let it be! Eleanor Roosevelt once said that no one can make you feel inferior without your consent. In the healthy single-parent homes I have known, a strong parent decided that home would never be considered 'broken.' "

This means concentrating on your strengths, not your weaknesses. One example of strength is that single-parent families often have strong support among their members. Children are less likely to team up against the parent. Older children less frequently plot against younger children than in two-parent families. An older child will help a younger brother or sister learn to ride a bike. The big brother is patient and reassuring, but would he have been as helpful if his father had been available? Dolores Curran concludes that children in single-parent families are more "responsible." They step in to do chores and help solve family problems. They prepare dinner for their working mothers or get on with their homework without prodding.

Alice Peppler has devoted a chapter to ways that problems can be turned into opportunities for the single parent. She does not deny feeling overwhelmed about being all alone as mother, father, provider, and housekeeper.

But she says it is precisely when we feel the task is too big for us that we find our resources.

The greatest source of strength is God: "He will not fail you or forsake you" (Deut. 31:6; Heb. 13:5). We often discover God only when we run out of our own means of coping.

There are other resources. You may think at first that the children are a burden, standing in the way of your career, your social life, your leisure time. But children are not a problem; they are a reward! You will never regret any sacrifice you make for your children.

Ms. Peppler speaks of other resources she has discovered as a single parent:

1. Time heals; life may get worse for awhile, but eventually it will get better; readjustment always takes time.
2. I love my children and they love me.
3. My children are part of this new single-parent home. They are partners with me far more than they were in the past.
4. As partners, my children can share in the planning, working, and life-style of our new situation.
5. In sharing in the planning and working, my children and I have the opportunity to communicate. . . .

God is a resource. Your children are a resource. But there are also support systems outside your family that can provide what you most need. Being a single parent is not a lost cause.

Single-Parent Homes in the Bible

When Jesus began his public ministry, he made an appearance at his home synagogue on the Sabbath. He spoke with a new authority that the townspeople had never seen in him before. Those who heard him said, "Where did this man get this wisdom and these mighty works? Is not this the carpenter's son? Is not his mother called Mary? And are not his brothers James and Joseph and Simon and Judas? And are not all his sisters with us? Where then did this man get all this?" (Matt. 13:54–56).

It was unusual in those days to refer to a young man by the name of his mother, but Mary plays an important role in the Gospels. There is another scene when we are told that she and Jesus' brothers came calling for him. They were concerned about reports they had heard (Mark 3:31–35). Later she was one of the few women present as Jesus was dying on the cross (John 19:25–27). After his death, Mary was with the disciples in the upper room in Jerusalem (Acts 1:12–14). At least two of her other sons—James and Jude—became leaders in the early church.

I mention all this because there are strong indications that Joseph, Jesus' foster father, had died. He is never mentioned after an incident that occurred when Jesus was twelve years old (Luke 2:41–51). There is good reason to believe that Mary had been left a widow while she still had children at home. Jesus most likely grew into adulthood in a single-parent family. Mary lived to see her children grow up to places of leadership; she was not defeated by her circumstances.

There is also an interesting recorded reference in the last Epistle Paul wrote. It was written to Timothy, a younger minister. Paul referred to his faith, which "dwelt first in your grandmother Lois and your mother Eunice," and then added, "and now, I am sure, dwells in you" (2 Tim. 1:5). We do not know what role Timothy's father played in his life. His father was a Greek and did not share the ancient Hebrew faith. Timothy's mother was left alone to pass on her faith to her son. And it worked!

have been single-parent families throughout
Many of them have found the resources to sur-
e difficult times. God provides!

One of the great changes I have observed in the last
few years is the number of single-parent families who
have discovered that the church satisfies their need for
companionship and community. I remember a time
when single parents kept their distance from the local
church. They may have felt ashamed or unwelcome. But
today I know many congregations that actively provide
support for single parents. For example, youth minis-
tries offer a strong adult-male presence. Single parents
help other single parents, and they also find older
couples who make excellent substitute grandparents.

A Plan of Action

God is your greatest resource, and his church can help
you. I want to offer a five-point plan of action as you
face life as a single parent.

1. *Don't try to be both parents.* You will only destroy
yourself if you try to fill both roles. A mother decides
that since her son has no father, she will make it up to
him. She tries to play football with him, but only places
yet another burden on the child and hurts herself as
well. This advice is not easy to accept, but do not think
that your heroic efforts will help you be both parents.
Trust God, your friends, and others to have a role in the
welfare of your children.

2. *When you have done your best, do not give up on
yourself because of guilt.* Either in trying to save a
faltering marriage or striving to be a good parent, all of
us fall short of the ideal. Even if you know that you are
guilty in a tragic way, you can make a new beginning
with God's help and forgiveness.

3. *Let your children be children.* It is tempting to
treat them as confidants to replace your departed

spouse. But, as much as possible, you owe it to your children to allow them to grow up in a normal way. Do not share with them information they cannot handle. Especially, if you feel bitterness over the marriage that has broken up, remember the child's best interests when you are tempted to list the faults of your ex-mate. Marie Winn has written a book entitled *Children Without Childhood*. She says: "Children today . . . are let in on the secrets of their parents' deficiencies, vulnerabilities, failings, weaknesses, long before these might become naturally apparent in the environment of an unbroken family."

Most young people learn slowly during adolescence that their parents are normal, fallible mortals. Little children who discover this suddenly find it hard to bear. The little child asks, "If my parents cannot take care of themselves, who will take care of me?" Don't deprive your child of a real childhood.

4. *Single parents must exercise consistent discipline.* A mother left alone cannot say, "Wait until your father hears this." There is no one else around to "handle this one." But your children need boundaries. You may often feel like giving up, especially when adolescent children are involved. But an adolescent will eventually become a mature adult if given guidance and discipline.

5. *A single parent must involve himself or herself with a circle of friends.* "Bear one another's burdens," the Bible says (Gal. 6:2). Acquaintances who have experienced your burden can help you sort out your feelings. You also need a time to relax and become refreshed. Include trusted friends in your support system and find opportunities to expand your horizons and social contacts.

15

What Really Matters in Building Your Marriage

Despite the disconcerting reports one hears about marriage failures today, there are bright rays of hope. Many people are concerned enough to want to do something about preserving their family relationships. Thousands of people each year go to marriage-enrichment seminars. Judging from the number of fine books and films on the subject of marriage, there must be millions of people who are not willing to sit by and watch their partnership fail.

What does it take to make a good marriage? We have concentrated on a few crucial areas: deep commitment to one another; free-flowing communication; a central value system, specifically, Christian values; satisfying intimacy; and caring cooperation in parenting tasks. Marriage manuals often include other concerns: money management; a positive relationship with the in-laws; and agreement on the roles of husband and wife.

All of these considerations are important. However, many of the marriage handbooks leave out the most important aspect of all. Unless the bride and groom agree on where their marriage starts from and is going, they will miss the one thing that can make a marriage happy.

Building Marriage on Romance

In *Fiddler on the Roof* one of Tevye's greatest concerns is the fact that his three daughters have reached the age for marriage. And that is the beginning of Tevye's troubles! For generations in the village of Anatevka, marriages had been arranged by the matchmaker. Tevye and his wife recall in a song how they first saw each other on their wedding day. Golde remembers that her mother and father had told her they would *learn* to love each other.

Things were very different for Tevye's daughters. They had minds of their own. They would not settle for the matchmaker's work. For their generation, love came before marriage. The girls had their eyes on young men who appealed to them. In marrying for love, they broke with the old tradition of arranged marriages.

That story represents the way people lived all over Europe until the last hundred years or so. Marriages are still arranged today in some cultures. Now we and our children shudder at the idea of marrying for anything other than love. Modern love stories give us the model: two strangers meet, fall in love, and live happily ever after.

The French writer Denis de Rougemont makes a startling observation in his *Love in the Western World*. He says there is a direct correlation between the high divorce rate and the fact that we "marry for love." He goes even further to say that the more we build our marriages on love, the shakier is the marriage. In the old days, when marriages were arranged, the divorce rate was very low. Today, romantic love is the basis of marriage, and the relationships often break apart.

There are two reasons why this is true. First, C. S. Lewis was correct when he said that *eros*—what we call attraction or falling in love—can unite people who are not suited for each other. An outsider can use all the powers of persuasion to convince two people who are "in love" that it will never work, but the advice will go unheeded. As Lewis says, a young man is most likely to conclude, "Better to be miserable with her than to be happy without her." They may be unsuited for each other by temperament, age, or background, but there is no convincing argument against "being in love."

John Fowles's *The French Lieutenant's Woman* developed this theme. A young man is about to marry a fine woman. Every possibility exists for them to make a happy marriage; they share a common background and education. Then the young man, against all reason, is drawn to a mysterious young woman of the town. He becomes so overwhelmed by his attraction for her that he ruins his plans for marriage.

This suggests a second reason why marriages based on romantic love alone have a higher failure rate. There was a key ingredient in those earlier marriages that is often missing today. For centuries, people married someone who shared a similar background and the same goals in life. The couple came from a common religious heritage and already accepted the same values. They found it simple to grow together instead of drifting apart.

It is surprising that marriages in our culture succeed as often as they do. We meet casually, date, become very serious, get engaged and then marry. But most people are so young when this process occurs. All that seems to matter is that they love each other. Subjects such as religion and moral values are very remote to many young people today. Their greatest dream may be nothing more than to fulfill in their own lives what they have seen enacted in the movies.

One of Tevye's daughters falls in love with a young revolutionary. Another loves a man who does not share her faith. As we watch the play, we catch the sadness in Tevye's eyes as he tries to understand this new world where love is supposed to be the one foundation on which a marriage stands. One daughter chooses a terribly difficult life for herself; her revolutionary husband is sent to Siberia. Another has become estranged from her family by marrying outside her religion.

There is one thing the play never tells us. It comes to an end as the daughters begin their struggle to maintain their marriages, far away from those who might have supported them. Was love enough to hold their marriages together? Will they have the happy home in middle age that Tevye and Golde have? The answer is left to our imagination. But one thing is clear: they pay a heavy price for this kind of marriage, where they do not have their faith and family to support them.

H. Norman Wright suggests in *The Pillars of Marriage* that no marriage can flourish when it is built on one thing alone. Even intense romantic love is not enough to serve as the foundation for a lifelong relationship. One marriage counselor has suggested that marriage is like a house with several support walls. We might call these walls love, communication, parenthood, and the resolution of conflicts.

I am suggesting that we take the analogy one step further. When the builder begins to erect a house, he has a very clear idea of what the building is meant to look like when finished. Just as the builder has plans and diagrams, marriage needs its common values and goals.

Marriage as a Means of Discipleship

The Gospels tell us in several contexts the cost of following Jesus. The original disciples left their nets and other occupations to follow him. They also left behind mothers, fathers, and families.

Jesus insisted that the kingdom was ultimately more important than even family. On one occasion Jesus said to a man, "Follow me." He responded, "Lord, let me first go and bury my father." Jesus replied, "Leave the dead to bury their own dead" (Luke 9:59, 60). Jesus was saying in a shocking way what he affirmed in another context: "He who loves father or mother more than me is not worthy of me..." (Matt. 10:37). Following Jesus often involved a break with the family.

Yet this is not the whole story. Soon after Jesus gave his hard words on the demands of discipleship, he was asked the question, "Is it lawful for a man to divorce his wife?" Jesus was being tested. His questioners wanted to know what marriage had to do with following Jesus. Jesus replied, "What therefore God has joined together, let not man put asunder" (Mark 10:2, 9).

Our commitment to Jesus Christ affects our marriages. The life of discipleship does not consist only in heroic acts. Following Jesus involves more than a martyr's death or one great moment of sacrifice. We follow Jesus every day—by the way we keep our promises and make our marriages work.

The Gospel of Luke uses a single word that throws much light on what discipleship means. All the Gospels speak of the disciple who takes up his cross to follow Jesus. Luke tells us that Jesus referred to those who take up the cross "daily" (Luke 9:23). This one word reminds us that we follow Jesus in all the little decisions we make each day—even in the way we react to our own mates and children.

Enrichment seminars and books can help improve marriage relationships. But the healthiest marriages are not always those in which all of the best psychological techniques have been applied. In the strongest marriages, two people are on a journey together. It is a pilgrimage of following Christ wherever he may lead them.

On this pilgrimage, you learn that something is more important than your own happiness. As you learn the fine art of caring for another person, you discover a love which becomes richer along the way. But the two of you are not simply gazing at each other; you have your eyes on the will of God as the goal for your lives.

C. P. Snow observed, "The pursuit of happiness is a most ridiculous phrase: if you pursue happiness you will never find it." He had a point. Those who constantly ask themselves, "Am I happy?" are not likely to find happiness. Jesus taught that only those who are ready to lose their life will find it (Mark 8:35). Marriage needs a goal beyond itself to give real meaning to the relationship.

Elizabeth Achtemeier stressed in *The Committed Marriage* the effect of discipleship on daily life in the family, from the breakfast table to the bedroom. Then she paraphrased 1 John 4:20: "If anyone says, 'I love God,' and hates his spouse, he is a liar; for he who does not love his spouse whom he has seen, cannot love God whom he has not seen." In our homes we indicate what we have learned from Jesus Christ.

A Shared Faith

Howard and Charlotte Clinebell wrote in *The Intimate Marriage*, "Shared meanings feed intimacy in a relationship; major differences in philosophy of life tend to lessen closeness. . . . when there are deep disagreements about the core meanings of existence, a couple must work doubly hard to establish creative closeness."

The authors conclude that the couple who shares a faith is fortunate indeed.

We cannot return to the world of the matchmaker in the small village as it is described in *Fiddler on the Roof*. But we would do well to discover one thing that world had going for it then. It usually brought together people who shared similar views about what is important in life. Marriages today are often made before the couple considers what their ultimate values in life are.

Many people find themselves already in a marriage where these important issues were not discussed. It is never too late to ask questions about your values. If goals have not been worked out and the place of religion in strengthening marriage has not been considered, begin to ask the questions now. If you want a healthy marriage, you will find that the greatest marriage enrichment of all is hearing Jesus' call to follow him. The strongest bond in marriage is a shared faith in Christ's leadership.